...urement wasn't taught when ...uilt the pyramids – was it?

Mark Baxter, Eamonn Leddy, Liz Richards, Alison Tomlin,
Topo Wresniwiro and Diana Coben

CONTENTS

www.nrdc.org.uk/measures

This report is funded by the Department for Education and Skills as part of *Skills for Life*, the national strategy for improving adult literacy and numeracy skills. The views expressed are those of the authors and do not necessarily reflect those of the department.

Preface

'Measurement wasn't taught when they built the pyramids': Enid, an adult numeracy student, used the Egyptians as an example when commenting on the place of common (standard) measures. She was wrong: for as long as we have records, measures have been at the heart of mathematics, and mathematics was taught in the Egyptian society which built the pyramids. We have chosen our title because it reflects the tensions between measures as used in society and measures in the curriculum.

Peer review

This report was read and critically peer-reviewed by: Paul Hamley, Further Education National Training Organisation; Anne Lee, Trades Union Congress; Tamara Bibby, Institute of Education, University of London; and Sue Gardener, National Institute of Adult Continuing Education.

Key points

Measures are a cornerstone of mathematics and of our lives: it is difficult to think of anything that is not measured. Despite this, there has been little research into the teaching and learning of measures, in school or adult education.

Most of the student participants had little practical need for formal measures, but nevertheless wanted to gain skills in order to be successful in mathematics examinations and to help their children. On the other hand, a minority had considerable skills, often beyond what was expected in the adult numeracy core curriculum, and usually gained through work rather than education. We found too that the language of measurement is extraordinarily rich but also ambiguous and complex.

The teachers, too, were frustrated. Too much work on measures, an apparently practical area of mathematics, was not about the process of measuring, but about converting between units, or calculations with little obvious purpose.

The team developed rich problems which support collaborative work and discussion, and the development of mathematical awareness and critical approaches to problems. They were tried out both in the teachers' classrooms and in an open seminar. Students valued time spent debating ways to solve problems, as well as practical measuring where they had a sense of a genuine problem - something they wanted to solve, or understand. The problems are not designed to be practical in the sense of mirroring life outside the classroom, but rather to be mathematically rich, interesting and supporting discussion.

It is not easy to sustain such approaches in the contexts in which the teacher-researchers worked: Further Education and prison, with achievement targets, set curricula and examinations and little time for teachers to develop their work. The report challenges some of the claims made by and for the adult numeracy core curriculum (in England), including its notions of the learner's context and the relationship of context to mathematics.

The report draws on team members' accounts of their work to discuss the satisfactions and difficulties of teacher research, and we also consider wider questions of the status of teacher research.

1 Introduction

This report describes the workings and findings of the National Research and Development Centre for Adult Numeracy and Literacy (NRDC) teacher-researcher project: *Teaching and learning common measures, especially at entry level*, conducted over nearly two years, from 2002 to 2004. The project was established by the NRDC, which has sought to raise the level of research and development for adult numeracy in England. This was the brief for the project:

The project's overall aim was to establish the features of successful learning and teaching of measurement, especially at entry level.

Specific objectives were:

1. To investigate the learning of measures, especially at entry level through:
    a)   eliciting and analysing learners' accounts of their learning; and
    b)   teacher-researcher/fieldworkers' observations of their students learning.
2. To identify teaching strategies to help adults learn measurement, especially at entry level through trialling and evaluating different approaches.
3. To produce and trial supporting learning materials.
4. To build research capacity through the use of teacher-researchers/fieldworkers.

Research questions:

- What are the key features of the learning of common measures especially at entry level?
- What are the key features of the teaching of common measures especially at entry level?
- What materials assist learners to learn common measures especially at entry level?

It seemed a straightforward brief, but as we worked on the project we found ourselves presented with new questions. One of our concerns throughout was the relationship of measures to the rest of the curriculum and to mathematics; and thinking about the place of measures in mathematics led us into discussions about the relationships between mathematics itself, the social use of measures and mathematics education.

Students told us about their use of measures inside and outside the classroom, and their purposes in studying mathematics. That led us to the mismatches and overlaps between two worlds: the skills, knowledge and view of mathematics identified with the curriculum, and students' knowledge and skills gained outside formal education and often barely acknowledged within it. Despite what sometimes seemed contradictions between students' practical interests and skills and the requirements of the curriculum, the students were positive about their studies. Measurement is 'practical' not only in the most obvious sense (knowing a baby's weight, for example, or calculating an estimate for carpet laying) but exactly because it is included in mathematics curricula: to help your child at school or to pass mathematics examinations yourself you need to deal with particular forms of measures. That led us to further concerns, to do with those particular forms. How can the skills of measurement be developed or tested in paper-based work? There is, too, a much wider question. Policy-makers see numeracy as one of the *Skills for Life* (DfES, 2001); are the skills chosen for inclusion in the core curriculum the most appropriate ones?

Meanwhile, we found that the immediate contexts for classroom work were sometimes strongly influenced by matters outside students' or teachers' control. Timetabling, classroom resources, initial assessment procedures, course organisation and particular forms of accountability all contributed to determining which students attended the courses and constrained teachers' ways of working.

Although measures have always been included in mathematics education, we found little prior research to guide us. Further, the methodology of teacher research is underdeveloped and so we considered not just how to collect and analyse data but a wider view of the meaning and status of teacher research (this is discussed in appendix 4).

These extensions to the original research brief are not neatly fenced off from each other. Our research questions, as laid out in the brief for the project, were straightforward but to respond only to them would have meant ignoring the complexities we uncovered during the project. Where possible we have tried to integrate our account of what happened – a teacher's lesson plan, a student's question in the classroom, students' accounts in interviews, our own explorations of the issues raised – with insights gained through our reading of policy and research. Where our starting points are more theoretical, we have sought to hold them up against students' and teachers' accounts.

1.1 Outline of the report

In section 2 we describe our starting points: the students, sites and courses. We also introduce the question of numeracy levels ('entry level 3' for example). In section 3 we turn from our classrooms to the background to our particular topic: *What is measurement, and why be interested in it?* We discuss the meanings of measures and consider previous research on the teaching and learning of measures.

We then, in section 4, tell the story of the project: explaining our reasons for choosing a case-study approach; students' participation; and our methods for gathering and analysing data.

Sections 5 and 6 are the heart of the report. In section 5 we ask: *What's the problem?*, from the perspectives first of students and then teachers. We finish section 5 with further discussion of the relationship of measures and mathematics, in the light of students' and teacher-researchers' comments.

In the second year of the project we concentrated on responding to the issues we had found. We developed new (to us) approaches to teaching measures, discussed in section 6. We describe what happened when students tried out classroom teaching and learning materials, and, drawing on interview and classroom data, discuss what seem to be great gains but also some difficulties in using such approaches. We also outline other resources developed by the team, which, like the materials, are available on the NRDC website.

The core team was made up of a researcher and four teacher-researchers (see appendix 5). In section 7 the teacher-researchers discuss their own experiences of the project, and we outline some practical issues for future teacher-research projects.

In section 8 we relate the project's work to the worlds of policy and management. In section 9 we draw together the implications of our research project for practice, policy and research.

2 Starting points: the students, sites, and courses

In this section we describe the immediate contexts in which we worked. Our own experience includes reading research and policy papers and reacting against them because they appear to generalise too readily, so we have sought to give enough information to enable readers to relate our research to their own settings. On the other hand, some readers may find such detail unnecessary to the main arguments, and wish to skim over the detail of course organisation in section 2.1 and return to closer reading in section 2.2, where we discuss the implications of course levels for our project. The project was established to study the teaching and learning of measures at entry levels, and we worked in appropriate classrooms – but we found both that students' skills did not neatly fit into levels and that for many numeracy education was not their prime aim – much less the study of measures. Section 2.2 therefore introduces some of the questions relating to policy which we later explore more fully.

The project had its life within the teacher-researchers' day-to-day work contexts. It is important to note that all the students with whom we worked were taking 'generic' numeracy courses – that is, not linked to specific contexts, such as family numeracy or particular workplaces or jobs.

2.1 Students and classrooms

In summary, the project worked mostly in two colleges of further education in inner-London and in two prisons, each for one year only. In the colleges the students were taking part-time courses, including 2.5 to 4.5 hours a week of numeracy, over an academic year and we worked with comparatively stable groups. In contrast, the prisons both had a high turnover of students, but differed in the feel of the education departments. In one prison, men could take about 10 hours a week of numeracy; in the other, the education programme was disrupted (in circumstances beyond the control of the education staff).

Here we outline the courses and the make-up of the student groups at the four main sites, and highlight some issues which may structure the students' (and researchers') experience of numeracy education. All the teacher-researchers and students worked to syllabuses delivering the adult numeracy core curriculum (ANCC). We hope these descriptions, of the further education (FE) colleges and then the prisons, will help readers contextualise the rest of this report.

2.1.1 The colleges

First we look at the two main college sites: Lambeth and Westminster Kingsway. Both are large (Lambeth has 20,000 students, or about 8,000 full-time equivalent) and serve mixed inner-city populations. With the near-disappearance of local education authority adult education in London, FE colleges have shifted from a central focus on post-school students to adults being the majority group (only 12 per cent of Lambeth's students are in the 16–19 age group). Both Lambeth and Westminster Kingsway College had several sites; here we outline numeracy courses at the two sites, in Brixton and Battersea respectively, where Liz and Eamonn, two of the project team, were based.

Lambeth College offered adult numeracy in: evening classes; part-time numeracy courses of eight hours a week; and full-time (15 hours) courses (usually over four days a week) combining literacy and numeracy. The part- and full-time courses included computer-assisted learning, cultural studies, progress reviews and tutorials; the numeracy strand was four and a half hours of both courses. Students just wishing to attend literacy or numeracy alone were often encouraged to attend the combined literacy and numeracy courses; and sometimes the choice of course was determined by the days on which they were able to attend college. Students were given a literacy and numeracy assessment and for the full-time courses were grouped by their literacy level. If there was more than one group at a particular level, numeracy was taken into account; but inevitably some numeracy groups were very mixed. Courses for 16 to 18-year-olds were organised separately at a range of levels.

In the first year, three groups of students participated in the project: an entry level 3 part time (eight hours) numeracy group, and two level 1 groups: 16–18 and adult, both full-time (15 hours) courses. The entry level 3 group had eight students (five men and three women); two of the students had been educated overseas and three were bilingual. The youngest student was 19 and the oldest in his late 40s. The 16–18 level 1 group had 11 students (four women and seven men); two had been educated overseas and two were bilingual. The level 1 adult group had 12 students (11 women and one man), mostly in their late 20s and early 30s; nine had been educated overseas and eight were bilingual. In the second year the project worked with an entry level 3 full-time group of eight students (two women and six men). All had been educated overseas, and two were bilingual. They ranged in age from 17 to 57. Adult numeracy students at Lambeth took the City & Guilds 3792 Adult Numeracy certificate at the appropriate level; the 16–18 groups were entered for level 1 Key Skills Application of Number.

At Westminster-Kingsway College there were no discrete basic skills classes or evening numeracy classes. Students enrolled termly on an adult Return to Study (RTS) course: four days per week with some 15/16 hours a week of programmed study comprising literacy, numeracy (two sessions per week, totalling two and a half or three hours), an IT session, tutorial time and some vocational taster classes. As at Lambeth, some students had access to additional learning support on a 1:1 basis or through a support tutor in the classroom. Most of the RTS students had initially applied for other courses in the college (particularly Access courses preparing for higher education) but were rejected and referred to RTS courses to improve their English and/or mathematics skills. A small number were referred on internally from groups for students with learning difficulties or from ESOL courses.

In both year 1 and year 2 of the project, Eamonn worked with groups designated as entry level 3 (E3). In year 1, there were 15 students (11 women, four men). Five of the students had at least some school education in London; others had their school education overseas (including the Caribbean, South America, the Asian sub-continent and Somalia). For six of the students English was an additional language (three had attended ESOL courses). Most were in their late 20s to early 40s, with two younger and two older. One student had severe visual impairment, and one had learning difficulties. The students were entered for the City and Guilds 3792 Adult Numeracy Certificate.

In year 2, there were 12 students (eight women, four men), aged 20 to 50, and with a mix of backgrounds and languages similar to the year 1 group. One student had no secondary school experience, and one had mild learning difficulties. Two of the students had good mathematics skills, but were less fluent in English. The students were entered for Edexcel adult numeracy certificates.

During the life of the project, Westminster Kingsway College announced that the building which housed their course was to be closed. We are grateful to the students for maintaining contact with the project despite uncertainty about their future studies. They raised the issue with Alison Tomlin:

Walanwal: So what's going to happen when this college close down then? ... [I'm] in a bit of a limbo.

Alison: Some of the students are really up and down. I can't do anything about it, that's the trouble.

Walanwal: You can put it in your report though, can't you?

The pedagogical approaches in Lambeth and Westminster Kingsway were broadly similar: Liz and Eamonn centred lessons on a topic, with a mix of whole group, small group, pairs and individual work within that. The materials were a mix of worksheets (often written by the teacher) and other tutor-made materials. Planning incorporated reference to the students' individual learning plans (ILPs) and to the core curriculum for adult numeracy (DfES & Basic Skills Agency, 2001a).

2.1.2 The prisons

The two prisons in which teacher-researchers worked, Brixton (Mark Baxter) and Belmarsh (Topo Wresniwiro), were dissimilar in many ways, but we start with what they shared. Both are prisons for men, with a wide range of ages, languages and experience of education. Belmarsh is a high-security dispersal prison but also a local and remand prison. Brixton is a category B local prison holding convicted and remand prisoners.

The average amount of time spent by inmates in HMP Brixton was two months; half of Belmarsh's inmates were on remand, and of those, 75 per cent left within six weeks. Education at Brixton was contracted out to Reed Learning, and at Belmarsh to Amersham and Wycombe College, which until May 2002 also had the Brixton contract. In both prisons, education policies were strongly influenced by the government's Offenders' Learning and Skills Unit (formerly the Prisoners' LSU), which has responsibility for national prison education strategies and sets targets for achievements. Both prisons offered a range of courses, together including art, cookery, pottery, music, social studies, Afro-Caribbean studies, IT, literacy and ESOL, and both had a dedicated numeracy classroom.

HMP Belmarsh
In Belmarsh lessons were packed, with around 10 students in a comparatively small room. Men were allowed up to five periods per week in any one subject (about 10 hours). Thus most students had fairly intensive numeracy tuition: several hours a week, but over a shorter period than a college's year.

A high proportion, perhaps half or more, of the students we met in Belmarsh were self-employed or casual workers, including painters and decorators, builders, gardeners and market traders. The range, however, was wide: one was a merchant banker. Around 60 per cent were in their mid-30s. Classes typically included students working at all levels of the core curriculum, sometimes joined by students taking the Open University mathematics foundation course. New students had a brief discussion with Topo Wresniwiro before completing a diagnostic assessment (designed by Topo). Most of the students were working at around entry level 3, though the research team noted that entry level 3 students in Belmarsh seemed to have more advanced skills than the entry level 3 students in college. This may be a practice developed within prison education: it is not easy for teachers or students to plan long-term developmental programmes of work. Mark suggested, in the context of HMP Brixton, that students may also undersell their skills, in order not to stand out, or to make sure they get a class place.

The men followed individual programmes of study, but often collaborated and the atmosphere was usually one of cheerful mutual support. Most students worked individually or in small groups, with some whole-group discussion, and the resources were similar to those in the FE colleges. Whereas Liz and Eamonn, in FE colleges, knew whom to expect at each lesson, Topo was given a list of students attending only 15 minutes before each class started.

Numeracy was organised, then, largely as individual work but in a supportive atmosphere, typically with Topo endeavouring to offer support at a range of numeracy levels and to people with varied interests, within the framework of the core curriculum but also extended above level 2. In one lesson, Alison talked with John White. He was a traveller, aged 21, who had recently transferred from a youth offenders' institution in Ireland where he had been taught numeracy for the first time. John had passed a fork-lift test in his last institution, and looked to that as a way to get employment when he left prison in three weeks. This was his second numeracy class in Belmarsh. He had never been to school, and said he was unable to read. He had good mental skills in addition and subtraction, but did not recognise the + and − symbols. At the same session Alison met Simon Bridge, who described his method to find the area of a circle (discussed below). Others in the group joined the discussion, and Topo picked it up and did some work on the board comparing the area given by Simon's method with that found by using the standard formula. Four or five of the students engaged enthusiastically with the discussion, using calculators to compare results; meanwhile, John looked lost, unable to follow the written work on the board, and told Alison it was a waste of his time to be there. At a later visit, John was confidently working through his own calculations, chatting with other students and cheerful about his progress. The students and tutor together had generated a collaborative culture despite the difficulties of working across such a wide range.

HMP Brixton

Five months into the *Measures* project Mark left HMP Brixton. On Alison's visits, she only once saw a lesson in progress: at other times men were held in the wings, or taking a numeracy examination (Baxter, 2003). Hence we collected comparatively little data about the teaching and learning of measures. Here Mark describes the numeracy provision.

> *In the year April 2002 to March 2003, the PLSU [Prisoners' Learning and Skills Unit] set these targets for HMP Brixton: 100 passes at level 2, 25 passes at level 1, and 25 passes at entry level. Education was very much focused on attaining targets which were looking for achievement at the higher levels of the core curriculum. Inmates would be given more attention if they showed the ability to pass level 1 and 2 examinations as soon as possible.*

> *In November 2002 the amount of education an inmate was entitled to in a week was reduced from 20 hours to 10 hours. Classes were not compulsory, although there was a suggestion at one point that men should only be allowed to apply for work if they passed a level 1 examination but this was never implemented. At that time men were paid 50 pence for attending a two-hour class, £3 for passing an entry level or level 1 exam and £5 for level 2.*

Men who wanted to study at a higher level could apply for distance learning packages. For their fees to be paid, however, they had to prove that they were going to be at Brixton prison for at least one year (requiring negotiation with prison, as well as education, staff).

Men applying for education would have to take an initial assessment. The reasons for this were not clear. The classes were mixed ability and the initial assessment results did not reach the tutors until after men started attending classes. However, there was often a great discrepancy between a man's initial assessment and his performance in class. When inmates were questioned these were typical responses:

You don't understand prison. If you show that you can read and write and do maths then you won't get any education.

(This was far from a correct perception. The higher you scored in your assessment the quicker you would get snapped up by basic education to be coached to do exams.)

Why should I make an effort when there's nothing in it for me?

The men had Individual Learning Plans but they were expected to go in the same direction which was the external examinations. They were slotted in at appropriate points in the schemes of work. They would be allotted to one of three schemes of work: working through the entry levels, or targeted at level 1 or level 2 examinations.

Broadly the schemes of work followed the core curriculum with the end result being the OCR examinations. In the early stages of the project the majority of the men in classes were working at levels 1 and 2, and their work on metric units followed on from sessions on decimals and was taught as a practical application of decimals. At one point a message came from a governor via the education manager that there should be no measurements made of classrooms and fixtures within it, and no teaching of map reading or maps and scales. No further action was taken when it was indicated that these topics were essential for exam work.

Basic skills classes were held in the education wing which required that prison officers would bring inmates from other wings. During this period the number of prison officers fell to such a level that delivery of inmates to classes was affected, so that gradually classes were rarely held in the education wing. By March 2003 it could not even be guaranteed to have men delivered for exams. Most education took place informally out in the wings. Men would work independently in their cells. Communication with tutors would be one to one, either out on the landings or shouting through the cell doors. There was an emphasis therefore on written explanations and materials which was a disadvantage to slow readers – but then they would not be part of our level 1 and level 2 cohort.

When many classes started to be cancelled, education was focused on men who could be entered for level 1 and 2 exams within two or three weeks. Such time constraints would imply that the purpose of the maths class in the main was to reinforce and revise existing skills rather than to establish underpinning skills. When I raised this with an inspector his reply was that in the time available my only realistic task was to introduce men to education in as positive light as possible in preparation for longer periods of education in other prisons. Work handed out on the wings tended to be more paper-based and because of the pressure to get men through exams and the nature of the core curriculum the work tended to be rather a lot about converting units, whereas in practical applications conversions are a smaller part. Men were supplied with paper rulers that could be slid under their cell doors. There was no work using weighing scales or measuring jugs as would happen in a college (though some inmates with drugs convictions already had experience of weighing in imperial and metric units to high levels of accuracy).

It was possible for men to pass the exams without ever seeing a measuring instrument. Of course in practical-based tasks this would have been impossible and maybe there are implications here about the purposes of including measurement in the core curriculum: What is it? What is it for? And therefore what are you going to examine?

Men's reasons for attending education courses varied. Attendance in class, tutor reports and examination results were all useful for parole applications. Inmates would often say they wanted to keep their minds occupied, and it was a relief from boredom. It was a reason to get out of their cells. I often heard what I had thought was a rather archaic phrase: "To better themselves".

We can compare Mark's account with that of Ade, a prisoner on the receiving end of the testing regime Mark describes. He talked to Alison while waiting for his third examination in three weeks (entry 1, 2 and now 3). The first exam was

really easy ... I haven't had a maths class, I just started straight on exams. I put in for IT and maths – maybe after you cope with the exams they'll put you into different groups.

Alison asked him what he thought of the exams:

A lot of it I've done already, it's second nature. I'm not sure if I've improved a lot – a few things I already knew. I learned a few things like fractions – when you leave [the exam] they give you a revision sheet and I go through that. I've done fractions before but it's a reminder. The sheets are not too hard and they gave a few examples, so I could get through some of it, not all of it.

The 'revision sheets' were worksheets, from Mark: they were the only form of teaching available to Ade.

Duffy, Dutch and Peter had been in the prison longer:

Duffy   *Mark makes an effort to train us up on our own. If you don't understand something there's no-one to ask, unless you has a cell mate or wing mate.*

Dutch   *It's putting pressure on Mark. He has to leave his base almost every day. It's his goodwill to give us things to do.*

Duffy   *He have to search for you.*

Alison described the government's expansion of numeracy education.

Dutch   *What the government says, it's a lie. In this prison you have good teachers, great teachers, but in this prison they have to be hunting us down to find us.*

Peter   *To further your education you should move on to convicted prisons.*

Duffy   *Prison has opportunities for education – I want to use it. I want to achieve something. They offer it —*

Dutch   *— so we will grab.*

Neil   *It's like they put plates on the table with the food but you can't reach it. I stand at the holding area all morning – I stand there 45 minutes. They say the teacher [Mark] don't come! And I say that is a man who come if he say he will come!*

In a sense this is none of our business (it's not about measures), but we have given this picture of educational life at HMP Brixton for two reasons. First, without insiders' accounts important issues may go underground. The examination results of prisoners like Ade from the period described above will go into the national pot and contribute to the overall record of achievement of targets within *Skills for Life*. Other organisations or individuals too may have supported students' evidencing of existing skills, rather than, or as well as, the development of new skills or understanding, in response to the pressure to meet targets and raise standards (as Mark put it: 'We're running out of people to put through the exams'). It may be that this period at HMP Brixton is a particularly sharp illustration of a wider problem. Our project was about practice in a particular section of the numeracy curriculum, but points to a need for wider research into the interface between policy and practice.

Our second reason is that we want to value Brixton inmates' contributions to the project. Despite their anger about their conditions of study the men were enthusiastic about their learning in numeracy and generous in their dealings with the research project. They wanted their views published. Dutch said:

All we said there [in Alison's notebook], we'd love it to go out.

Like work-based, community or FE provision, prisons and prison education departments differ. A teacher in a prison outside London described to us working in a much more stable environment where teachers and students could expect to have enough time together to be able to work in similar ways to FE, but with more available tuition time per week – that is, groups could potentially develop some cohesion and the curriculum could be seen as a whole.

2.2 Courses and levels: 'It's not like it's my choice'

Our project is unusual in working on a specific element of one of the *Skills for Life* curricula, at a limited range of levels: that is, we thought we had a neatly limited research field. However, as the project developed we found the apparent tidiness unravelling. Shifts in our ideas of what measurement means and its place in adult numeracy work will be discussed below. Here we outline another issue: the levels of courses and means of student referral.

Students in the FE colleges were assessed before placement in the most appropriate group.

However, with a limited range of numeracy provision in comparison with literacy and ESOL, students were usually grouped by their literacy and/or language skills rather than their numeracy skills. An 'entry level 3 numeracy course' might include a huge range of levels. Eamonn commented on referral processes at his college:

> Students were often placed in groups primarily according to their (English) literacy skills, resulting in very diverse numeracy classes. Even if a written initial numeracy assessment had been conducted, this often only scratched the surface of their knowledge and experience and could result in students with poor numeracy skills being placed alongside other very numerate students with poor language skills, and so on.

Thus Kamar, a Somali mathematics graduate, sought to improve her English for mathematics, with a view to becoming a primary school teacher. She attended a RTS course and was confident that it was appropriate for her even though her mathematics skills were far beyond those of her colleagues. Rosalie (Lambeth College) was content with the numeracy level, but said the IT element of her course was too advanced for her: 'We all have weaknesses and strengths but [I'm] like a slow runner trying to keep up with a fast one.'

A group of 16 to 18-year-old students in FE found themselves 'moved up' for numeracy because their literacy skills had improved. The class initially worked at entry level 3 in literacy and numeracy. As their literacy skills improved, the course level was raised during the academic year to level 1 – and they also had to attend level 1 numeracy classes. Mark met them when they had spent nearly an academic year working at too high a level. In the following year one of these students attended Mark's entry level 3 classes – that is, he dropped back down a level. Mark commented,

> He [...] tried hard but barely scraped a pass in the City and Guilds entry level 3 assignment. What had he been going through sitting in a level 1 class for nearly a year?

Here is Cartel, a student at Belmarsh, who had a GCSE grade C:

> Not that I'm interested [in mathematics] yeah, but when I come here, they just sent me to maths. I never chose the subjects as such, it's more they chose the subjects for me. ... Yeah, they gave me an assessment. They said I want to do maths, ... first day, that's where they sent me. So it's not like it's my choice.

There have never been as many students in adult numeracy as in ESOL (in some areas) and literacy. Numeracy is now a high priority subject and providers are encouraged to recruit as many students as possible. One means of expanding provision is to amalgamate numeracy with literacy as part of a combined course, as both the FE colleges had done. None of the students with whom we spoke resented being steered into numeracy – for example, Cartel went on to say that he had become interested in mathematics through attending the course – but the pressure for numbers forms the backdrop to our study.

Some – perhaps most – of the students with whom we worked had not initially requested numeracy. Further, we doubt that anyone specifically asked for work on measurement when they enrolled – so we studied something that was not the prime aim for students, but rather part of a larger project for them, for educational establishments and for the government.

2.3 Summary

We hope this outline of our contexts has given the reader some impression of the places and times from which students and the research team speak in this report. It will be clear that ours is a relatively small-scale study focusing on in adult numeracy provision in two different types of institutions (FE colleges and prisons) in a particular part of the country (London). The FE courses included 72 students, most of them attending for an academic year; in the prisons, the two teacher-researchers worked with about 20 students at entry level. Altogether, we had access to the work of more than 90 students working at, broadly, entry 2 to level 1. We make no claim that the contexts and students in our study are representative, but on the other hand there is no reason to think them particularly unusual.

3 What is measurement, and why be interested in it?

3.1 Measures are at the heart of mathematics

At first sight, it is foolish to ask why we should be interested in measurement. Everything in the world is measured now: global warming, kitchen units, changing tides, the distance to the moon, stock market movements, happiness... (cf. Johnston, 2002). Measurement is at the heart of mathematics, which **Chambers' Twentieth Century Dictionary** (Geddie, 1964) defines as 'the science of magnitude and of number, and of all their relations': measurement is a foundation stone of mathematics. It exists in all human cultures as one of the six pan-cultural mathematical activities identified by Alan Bishop, along with counting, locating, designing, explaining and playing (Bishop, 1988). The influential Cockcroft Report states that 'it is possible to summarise a very large part of the mathematical needs of employment as "a feeling for measurement."' (Cockcroft, 1982, p.85).

However, despite its importance, there is relatively little published research on the teaching and learning of measurement, especially with respect to adults (FitzSimons & Godden, 2000). What relevant research literature there is is summarised here under the following headings: studies of adults' use of measurement, and studies of learning and teaching measurement.

3.1.1 Adults' use of measurement

Measurement has been considered as a social practice and investigated by several researchers in different contexts (Johnston, 1999; Lave, 1988; Nuñes, Light et al. 1993). In her influential study of 'situated cognition', Jean Lave observed members of a Weight Watchers club preparing meals for themselves in their own kitchens (Lave, 1988). She found that calculation of measured quantities was only one element in their everyday activities, and that it was often not necessary to be exact; it was enough to have an idea of quantities being larger or smaller. The weight watchers often developed their own systems of measurement, disregarding what they had been taught in the club.

Workplace studies have shown the importance of measurement in a range of industrial contexts. Gail FitzSimons demonstrated how Bishop's six pan-cultural mathematical activities occurred amongst workers in a pharmaceuticals factory in Australia. She noted, with respect to measuring and counting, that orders needed to be made up with due regard for fragility and temperature sensitivity and that records needed to be made, checked and rechecked throughout the production process (FitzSimons, 2000, p.144). Terezinha Nunes Carraher investigated the use of scalar relationships in building work in her article, 'From drawings to buildings: Working with mathematical scales' (Carraher, 1986). Robyn and Kelly Zevenbergen (2004) studied the numeracies of young boat-builders in Australia, and found that while minimal mathematics was being used in the workplace, 'estimation, holistic thinking, problem solving, informal measurement and aesthetics were dominant processes used by employees'. They quote the following exchange to illustrate the workers' use of non-standard measures (in this case, fingers and pencils):

Tony: *We measure with everything. Like say, two finger gap there, same on that side, that's what I was using my pencil for as well trying to line up gaps like that.*

Interviewer: Fingers and pencils and all that sort of stuff.

Tony: *Yeah, well we don't always use a tape measure.*

In a study in Argentina, Juan Llorente analysed the process of making apple jam, as described by Mónica, a woman with little formal education (Llorente, 2000). Mónica described the ingredients in terms of their weight, gave an estimate of the length of time the apples need to cook before sugar is added ('more or less, two or three hours') and showed that she understood the principle of proportionality which is crucial to successful jam-making.

Interviewer: How much apple do you use?

Mónica: *Well, some three kilos of apples.*

Interviewer: And for that many kilos of apples, how much sugar do you use?

Mónica: *One and a half kilos if they are green, if they are red, one kilo, because the green ones are always more acid.* (Llorente, 2000, p.73)

Mercedes De Agüero reported on a study of an extended family group of painters in Mexico City, focusing particularly on their estimations of quantities and costs. She examined the relationship between group members' collective and individual problem-solving strategies, and their 'dynamic negotiation' between representations of work processes and internal operations within the work and the prevailing external conditions (de Agüero, 2003).

In these studies, the mathematics involved in these measurement activities is identified as such by the researchers; the adults whose activities they are investigating may not regard what they are doing as mathematics. This is in line with Lave's observation that problems in adults' lives which involve mathematics are structured in terms of the activity and its purpose for the adult concerned, rather than in terms of mathematics. Mathematics is thus rendered 'invisible' to those most closely involved in the activity (Coben & Thumpston, 1996; Noss, 1997). This tendency of mathematics to become invisible when it is embedded in artefacts and activities seems to apply across cultures, in very different societies. For example, Paulus Gerdes (1986; 1997), working with villagers in Mozambique, describes the mathematics 'frozen' in their cultural activities, artefacts and buildings, a point also made by Mary Harris (1997) in her celebration of the mathematics in crafts and other activities traditionally associated with women, many of which involve measurement. Meanwhile, in technologically advanced societies, Rudolf Sträßer has noted the disappearance of mathematics into modern technologies: specialists may use mathematics when the technology needs repair, but until that moment, the mathematics that makes the technology work is invisible to the user (Sträßer, 2003).

The tendency of mathematics to 'disappear' is shown in a different way in a study investigating the mathematics in adults' lives (Coben & Thumpston, 1996). Several people interviewed in the study dismissed as 'just common sense' the mathematics they could do, reserving the term 'mathematics' for what they could not do. One woman in the study, Eileen, used 'mathematics' in a different way. She distinguished between mathematics and 'non-mathematical mathematics', citing the example of her husband, a carpet-layer, who, she says, is very good at 'non-mathematical mathematics': 'he can look at a room and estimate the size of it and how much you are going to need' (Coben & Thumpston, 1996, p.293). While Eileen is talking about her husband's abilities rather than her own, the ability to measure is not necessarily seen as mathematical by those actually doing the measuring either. For example, the carpenters in Wendy Milroy's study in South Africa have a deep understanding of measurement but do not regard it as mathematics (Milroy, 1992). In our own study, an HMP Belmarsh prisoner, Mark, estimated (by eye) wall lengths and the amount of paint needed to paint the library. When Alison Tomlin commented on that involving mathematics, he said 'You're trying to make me sound brainy ... the questions you are asking is just general knowledge really'.

So should we describe such activities involving measurement as 'mathematical'? In doing so, are we imposing our view of what is and is not mathematical on measurement activities which those concerned see in other ways? Certainly Paul Dowling (1998) would say that we are; he warns against such interpretations as denying the activity as undertaken by the person concerned. In a similar vein, Ole Skovsmose (1994) describes the 'formatting power' of viewing the world through a 'mathematical lens'. Such interpretations have been criticised as tending to legitimise the school mathematics curriculum (Zevenbergen & Zevenbergen, 2004). The research team has struggled with this dilemma throughout the project, acknowledging that we are privileging one viewpoint over other possible interpretations. We have adopted Zevenbergen & Zevenbergen's partial solution: to ensure that the voices of participants (in our case, adult numeracy students) are strong in our account of our research.

It may also be important to look at situations where measurement might be expected to occur but is not used. For example, a study by Thomasenia Lott Adams and Gregory Harrell (2003) of estimation at work by 18 professionals found that: they often use more than one sensory skill to develop an estimate and use external sources to build or support their estimations; they may be very concerned about either underestimating or overestimating; real life estimation tasks are often multi-faceted. The researchers also asked participants in their study to give reasons for estimating and also for choosing to measure accurately. Six reasons for estimating were given: it saves time; it helps to verify the validity of measuring tools and methods; in some situations precise measurement may not be possible; estimation may be required by the nature of the job; customers may want estimates for the cost of specific tasks before the professional starts work, therefore accurate calculation is not possible; one participant said that he estimated because it was enjoyable. Four reasons for choosing not to estimate were given: estimation is not always possible, depending on the specific attribute to be measured; the customer may want a precise or consistent product; the risks and consequences of a mis-estimate may be serious; the professional may be unfamiliar or uncertain about the task at hand.

Experience seems to be an important factor here. For example, a study of workers in a carpentry workshop found that the more experienced ones were better able to do the calculations requiring measurement in their work, despite the fact that the apprentices had had more schooling. The researchers concluded that apprentices probably learn the mathematics they need gradually, through their experience of using the carpenters' lists of materials and measurements, rather than through their schooling (Nuñes, Schliemann et al. 1993). So what does research tell us can be done to encourage the learning and teaching of measurement? Here we focus especially, but not exclusively, on adults, although, as noted above, there is a paucity of adult-focused research literature on this topic.

3.1.2 Learning and teaching measurement

Gail FitzSimons argues for the use of Bishop's six pan-cultural mathematical activities, including measurement, as a basis for curriculum development and the development of a broader notion of occupational competence. She argues for vocational education to adopt a broad, research-based interpretation of the term 'mathematics', contending that such an approach 'would see mathematics as a central underpinning and integrative study for living and working in a technologised world.' (FitzSimons, 2000, p.224).

Myriam Steinback and her colleagues emphasise the importance of starting with students' understandings in their account of measurement in adult education (Steinback et al. 2003). They consider that the biggest challenge for teachers is to find ways of incorporating what learners already know about measurement, and about mathematics in general, into the mathematics classroom. They present 'vignettes' from two teachers' classes where meaningful mathematical experiences occurred and where adults' understandings about measurement became visible and audible, drawing out the implications for practice, alongside a vision of an ideal adult classroom and a review of relevant United States policy documents. They make the case for the use of real tools in the adult classroom and argue for the role of inquiry as a motivator. They stress the importance of the teacher making purposeful connections to adult learners' informal knowledge base.

Anne Abbott discusses her attempts to develop measurement skills in her class of adult learners of mathematics, most of whom have left school without adequate secondary qualifications and who are hoping to continue their education at tertiary level; the class included some who intend to enter nurse training. She notes that at the outset very few students recognised immediately that the smallest divisions in a 1000ml measuring cylinder were 10ml, not 1ml. One of the syringes had 0.2ml divisions, and most students did not realise that (Abbott, 2002). Abbott describes hers as a critical mathematics approach, along the lines described by Rachel Patrick (1999), with students working in groups through her worksheets setting out problems involving measurement. Their results in the final assessment showed a marked improvement on previous years.

The tools used for measurement feature in Poppy Pickard and Patricia Alexander's investigation of the effects of digital measuring equipment on concepts of number, reading of a number line and estimation from scales, of students in United Kingdom higher education (many of them adult returners); they compare their results with research undertaken in schools (Pickard & Alexander, 2001). They note that some students' errors seem to be the result of reading the digits but not reading the place value:

> *In other words they are looking for like digits and not like place or size. Another common error was the inability to accurately read the minor divisions. Sometimes a single minor division is ignored and estimation is undertaken in only one section. When four or nine minor divisions are used they can be attributed the wrong value, e.g. counted in twos instead of ones.* (Pickard & Alexander, 2001, p.145)

They conclude that the challenge for the teacher is to use technology not only as a computational device but also as a pedagogic device to enhance students' understanding of mathematics. Betty Johnston reminds us that this understanding should be critical:

Learning a craft involves not only skill with the tools, but knowledge of when to use them. Yes, let's teach people how to measure (and to count and to calculate), but let us ask also about the appropriateness of the measure, let us ask why, who and what we are measuring. (Johnston et al. 1997)

Research with children may also be relevant here. For example, in their article reporting on a study with children on the measurement of length and area, Terezinha Nuñes and her colleagues conclude that:

Simple measurement systems involve three basic operations. First, a unit which is conserved across time and space must be found. Second, it must be applied successively to the object when it is larger than the unit. Third, it must be systematically subdivided when there is no whole number that can fully cover the object. These basic operations are involved in both the measurement of length and area. (Nuñes, Light et al. 1993)

In designing teaching programmes, they advise teachers to introduce cultural practices that support children's intuitive approaches to measurement (Nuñes, Light et al. 1993).

But how intuitive are children's approaches to measurement? Douglas Clements (1999, p.5) describes the strong impression left on him when his 3rd grade (elementary) school pupils in the USA asked for more metre sticks in order to measure a room. After trying to get them to come up with a solution themselves using the sticks available, he suggested 'How about this? Can you lay a meter stick down, mark the end with your finger and then move it?'. Clements describes the pupils' response as surprised and enthusiastic: 'Wow! Good idea!', but he was concerned, reflecting afterwards, 'How could this be new to them?' It evidently was new to them. This is one of the obvious differences between teaching children (especially young children) and adults: adults have more experience of the world than young children and this experience is likely to include some experience of measuring things and of understanding that a measure can be used more than once in a given measurement activity.

Measurement involves both skill and understanding and Kay McClain and her colleagues (1999) describe how one group of 1st grade elementary school students in the USA developed personally meaningful ways to reason mathematically within the context of measurement. The activities included measuring by pacing, something which featured in our project also (see sections 4.2 and 6.1.2, below). They highlighted students' mathematical reasoning, noting the importance both of discussions in which students explain and justify their thinking and of carefully sequenced teaching activities. They conclude: 'The crucial norm that became established was that of explaining and justifying solutions in quantitative terms' (McClain, Cobb et al. 1999, p.105). Their conclusion supports the view that measurement should be integrated in the curriculum rather than treated as a separate area of teaching and learning, since pupils' abilities to reason quantitatively also improved:

the students' reconceptualisation of mathematics went hand in hand with their development of increasingly sophisticated way of reasoning. In particular, preliminary analysis of the data indicates that students who, at the beginning of the classroom teaching experiment, were unable to reason quantitatively with numbers up to 20 were, by the end of the experiment, able to reason in a variety of ways with numbers to 100. (McClain, Cobb et al. 1999, p.105)

3.2 Summary

So where does this brief review of research leave us? First, with a strengthened awareness of the paucity of research in this area: our study breaks new ground in examining in depth issues in teaching and learning measurement with adult students. Next, it raises questions about the organisation of the adult numeracy core curriculum which forms the curricular context of this study. The curriculum separates *Measures, shape and space* from *Number* and *Handling data*. It is built around a hierarchical structure, so that, for example, whole numbers are dealt with before fractions and decimal numbers. The effect may be that the place of measure at the heart of mathematics is lost. The research team found ourselves addressing questions relating to mathematics, rather than to numeracy as defined in the curriculum. The potential shown in McClain, Cobb et al.'s study for the beneficial effect on number work of increasing students' understanding of measurement is lost if measurement is not fully integrated in the curriculum.

Further, it reminds us of the importance of gearing teaching to students' experience and cultural practices that support their intuitive approaches to measurement. Units of measure may be informal and personal (the length of one's arm as a unit of measurement) or 'common' (standard); the curriculum proposes using informal measures only as a way in to understanding the importance of common measures. But measures of both kinds are always encountered, used and developed in context, whether that be examination-passing, banking, warfare, pleasure and creativity, helping one's children or in a particular workplace. The ANCC declares itself to be context-free while creating its own pedagogical context (course organisation, lesson plans, textbooks, software, examinations and targets).

Other questions are not covered in the research reviewed here, for example, the important issue (for our project) of level, a reflection of the paucity of research on the assessment of adult numeracy. Adult numeracy students in England are assessed at a particular level, calibrated against national standards (QCA, 2001) yet their skills, and their uses of mathematics, rarely if ever exactly fit that level. How does this complexity mesh with students' purposes, and how do students' purposes mesh with the curriculum? We know that students with 'spiky profiles' (DfES & Basic Skills Agency, 2001b) may already know and use mathematics that is 'beyond their level', or, to state the same point more negatively, they may have 'gaps' in their knowledge. (That idea of gaps seems only to apply at lower levels of mathematics: the top mathematicians in the world in the 1940s may only have known 10 per cent of the world's mathematics, and it's less now (Davis & Hersh, 1981), yet no-one worries about their spiky profiles.) Mathematics itself is complex, messy, limitless, beyond any single person's full understanding; the curriculum (perhaps necessarily) is assumed to be simplified by being rendered into elements and levels. Students, teachers and the research team were dealing with mismatches, overlaps and gaps.

4 The story of the project: student participation and analysing data

This report is the story of a case study undertaken in the qualitative research paradigm[1]. The following generally accepted characteristics of qualitative research (Merriam 1998; Guba & Lincoln, 1981) fit our project well:

- There is an overarching interest in understanding the meaning people have constructed.
- There is an inductive approach to generating knowledge.
- The researcher focuses on gaining the emic, or insider's perspective.
- Meaning is mediated through the researcher's own perceptions.
- The researcher is the primary instrument for data collection and analysis.
- The research design is emergent, flexible and responsive to changing conditions of the study in progress.
- The sample selection is usually non-random, purposeful, and small.
- The researcher spends considerable time in the natural setting of the study, often in intense contact with the participants.
- The end product is narrative and richly (or 'thickly') descriptive.

Within this general framework, the case-study method focuses on holistic description and explanation and has an interpretive epistemological orientation (Gall, et al. 1966). The aim of case study, which makes it particularly appropriate to our project, is to understand the meaning of a process or experience. Different types of case study are classified by Gall et al. (1966) by purpose, differentiated as: description; explanation; and evaluation. Robson (1993) adds a fourth purpose: exploratory, an approach which seeks to find out what is happening, to seek new insights, to ask questions, and to assess phenomena in a new light. Our project was descriptive in Gall et al.'s terms and exploratory in Robson's terms; it needed to be both, since so little previous work has been done in this area. Ours was also a multiple-case study, since the project covered several sites and contexts for learning and teaching. For multiple-case studies, Gall, et al. recommend reporting the results for each case, including sufficient 'thick' description to bring the case alive for the reader, and also providing a cross-case analysis, noting consistencies and differences in constructs, themes, and patterns across the cases; this we have done. Within the case studies, we used ethnographic research tools to collect data (Green & Bloome, 1997) and our data analysis methods are consistent with those of grounded theory (Eisenhart, 1988; Hillier & Jameson, 2003). We used QSR Nud*ist software, coding both for categories emerging from the data and for curriculum elements.

In this section we outline student participation, and how we gathered and analysed data.

4.1 Student participation

Following an induction day for the teacher-researchers, researcher and project director, the teacher-researchers spoke with students about participation in the project. We produced a

---

1 A more detailed account of theoretical and methodological issues in this study is available as a pdf on the NRDC website (www.nrdc.org.uk).

leaflet, distributed to students, outlining the project and the range of possible levels of involvement, from none, to full participation including being interviewed and tape-recorded (appendix 1).

The project followed the British Educational Research Association ethical guidelines (BERA, 2000), but we have found a lack of discussion of the rights of research participants in the action research and teacher research literatures. As the leaflet explained, teachers always keep records of classes; we said that the research team would not see notes about students who refused their participation. It was fortunate that all the students agreed to participate: had that not been so, we might have had difficulties making sense of classroom notes with some data omitted.

4.2 Gathering data: from scatty notes to taped interviews

We have said that only a minority of the teacher-researchers' classes included work on measures. The team kept notes both of classes which included work on measures and of other factors of working life relevant to the project, including the cancellation of classes, the ways in which students were referred to courses, time for preparation, and so on. Meanwhile, the researcher also observed 14 lessons (typically with eight–ten students) with the main focus on measures. Liz Richards describes the difficulty of gathering data in one's own classes in section 7 . Alison Tomlin too, even as an outside 'observer', was distracted by classroom life: 'Scatty notes because I moved around and did a fair bit of trying to help rather than note-taking' (on a visit to Westminster Kingsway College). We had hoped that the teacher-researchers would be able to visit each other's classes, but their teaching timetables made that impossible. They interviewed each other so that they had a better basis for comparing experiences.

Over the two years of the project, none of the students with whom we worked refused their permission for data to be collected about their classes, classroom discussions about measures or their individual work. As noted above, the FE courses included 72 students, most of them attending for an academic year; in the prisons, the two teacher-researchers worked with about 20 students at entry level. Altogether then, the research team had access to the work of more than 90 students.

Rather than approaching students individually to request interviews, we explained the project to groups of students during their class time and asked how they wanted to be interviewed (if at all). One FE class (Liz's 16–18 group) rejected the idea of any form of interview; the others opted for group or individual discussions (some students choosing not to be interviewed).

We tape-recorded conversations with a total of 47 students in individual or pair interviews and class discussions: across the project, two classes opted for a group discussion; 10 students gave individual interviews; and 17 were interviewed in pairs or groups of three. In addition, Eamonn Leddy discussed the language of measures with an ESOL class, and a communications teacher led a taped discussion about students' use of measures with one of Liz Richards's groups.

In the prisons we interviewed one student individually and 10 in small groups, taking hand-written notes only (we had permission for taping in one prison only, late in the project). This process produced very different data from the taped interviews. At the start of each discussion, Alison took notes as quickly as possible, and inevitably missed a great deal. At both Belmarsh and Brixton, the interviewees started to speak more slowly, checking that Alison was keeping up; the material has an edited feel to it, as students had time to organise their speech.

The interviews were semi-structured, with a choice of routes: one starting with the student's personal contexts (including their aims, their prior education and their needs, if any, for measures) and moving to discuss measures in particular, and the other starting from the student's present work in numeracy, including measures, and moving outwards. Some students spoke extensively about their experiences, opinions and advice, and we barely referred to the schedule, rather listening to their comments then checking for coverage of the issues at the end. Others read the schedules and told us which they preferred: 'I think, because we've been talking about measurement in class, for me, probably talking about measurement in class would be more of a progression' (Elizabeth, choosing the second route).

At the end of individual and group interviews, we asked if there were other questions we should have asked. We intended that as a way of improving the interview schedules, but it turned out to be a way for students to extend the present discussion. For example, Bob's question was this:

> How did anything in your past help in these days? What you did in the past, if you did anything educational in the past?

When Alison asked him his own question he talked about the previous educational centre he had attended. When we put Bob's question to Elizabeth, she first mentioned using fingers for multiplication, then added: 'I was going to say, in my mind what makes a good teacher is someone who tailors the lesson to the students they have', and went on to expand on that idea. In HMP Brixton a student asked: 'Should we get more pay? Education, isn't it?' – making the point that prisoners were paid more for work than for education.

Where possible, transcripts and/or tapes were returned to students, and they were advised they could change anything with which they were not content. Students were asked to choose their own pseudonyms. Some Brixton prisoners said we should use their real names because they wanted their arguments to be made openly, but we refused, because that might have exposed others.

Classroom notes and tape transcripts of group and individual discussions were our main data sources, but we also had additional material. Several students said they would keep diaries about their use of measures, but only four did so, as far as we know; in addition, two students gave us written accounts of a joint classroom project.

We lent out disposable cameras for students to photograph anything in their view to do with measures. We hoped that would be a way to move from the limitations of the curriculum to a wider view, but it seems it takes more than a camera to dislodge a curriculum-bound view of the meaning of measures. For example, Elizabeth took photos (including street signs and a water bottle) but said she had noticed them only because she was 'looking for' measurements. That is, the camera led her to see formal measures where before she had not noticed them, rather than helping the research team to 'see' students' uses of measures. It might be a useful strategy for teachers, but did not greatly help the research project.

A limitation of the project is that we worked exclusively with students who were reasonably content with their numeracy courses – at least, satisfied enough to continue attending and take part in the project. We wanted to encourage students to be critical, and with that in mind, produced a leaflet of quotations from students, selected to be as contradictory as possible to make it clear that alternative views were welcomed. We sometimes quoted particular comments to interviewees to try to generate debate. We cannot tell if this 'worked' since we do not know what would have happened in those interviews without using that method, but it was a vehicle for further discussion. For readers who would like a closer sight of our sources, samples of a range of interview data (from different interviewers, sites, means of recording and so on) are posted on the project website at www.nrdc.org.uk. As we used extracts from interviews to support further discussion with participants, so readers are welcome to use the website transcripts to start discussion in their own contexts.

In the second year of the project, we continued collecting classroom and interview data but also team members developed new teaching ideas, which were tried out by students and the teacher-researchers either in their own classes or at a half-day *Students' Seminar on Measurement*. The seminar was organised because we believed that to try out materials only in the teachers' usual classes would not generate a critical enough response: we imagined that perhaps the new ideas might be approved just because, as we said above, students were generally approving of their teachers' work.

We distributed a leaflet outlining the project and some tentative findings and inviting students to participate in planning a 'workshop' on measurement (appendix 3). Rose, Tony, Kamar and Walanwal, students at Westminster Kingsway College, responded and we organised two planning meetings at their college. They planned a half-day event, and wrote an invitation which was distributed to project participants and other South London centres where we had contacts:

> *The students of Westminster Kingsway would like to invite other adult students to a seminar on measurement … We are doing some activities to make it easy and interesting to do some measurement, and we want your help and advice. It is part of a research project on adult numeracy courses. Anybody interested, come along and bring your ideas with you! (Appendix 3)*

The seminar was held in March 2004. Twenty-six students came, mostly from colleges where teacher-researchers worked but also from two other South London organisations; from that event, we have a video tape, two audio tapes, photographs and hand-written notes. We moved the recorders around the two rooms we were using, but inevitably missed many of the discussions as students worked in small groups on different activities.

4.3 Dealing with the data

The teacher-researchers' and Alison's notes of classroom observations and all interview transcripts were distributed to all the team members. The team had 17 meetings, including one, at LLU+ at South Bank University (www.lsbu.ac.uk/lluplus), to survey teaching and learning materials. Our discussions ranged from the particular meanings of a set of notes to the overall parameters of the research. We illustrate this with an extract from the notes of our discussion of emerging themes, three months into the project:

Decimal numbers, place value central to team's concerns:

- Two different possible approaches: slog directly at the meaning of decimals, or get comfortable in contexts of practical applications, and then generalise from it.
- Is the problem in the decimal numbers directly, or in that the maths the students are engaged in shows up these issues?
- cf word problems (... and further issues relating to place value).

What is the difference between the measurement bit and the rest of the curriculum?

- Measurement is more concrete – people should be able to picture what the answer means.
- If people do not need measurement (many people say they do not do any measuring) then are we colluding in a reductive view of maths education?
- Need to pick up on what people can do that they don't call maths, and consider the question of who decides what is 'mathematics' and what is not.
- Basically patronising stance? Possibility that we, the curriculum, policy-makers all tend to look at the curriculum from a consumer point of view (the shopper, the person seeking best value, the person doing DIY) rather than e.g. the shopkeeper seeking to maximise profit?

Tick lists:

- One of the losses in the curriculum is that it fragments areas that once could be linked. We used to focus on making connections between areas of maths – e.g. topic-based work – but the need to tick off bits of the curriculum militates against that.
- Shift against trusting the teaching profession – the need to provide evidence for everything takes up teachers' time. (Research team minutes)

So team meetings were the focus for data analysis, discussion of issues and setting agendas for future work. The team's own concerns about the satisfactions, problems, inconsistencies and absences in their teaching became directly part of our data, as well as influencing the questions we sought to answer in the collection and analysis of data from students.

We gained new ideas through presenting our work at various conferences: two NRDC international conferences (Coben et al. 2004) and a teacher-researcher conference (London, 30 January 2004); Adults Learning Mathematics (ALM) – an International Research Forum (Baxter et al. 2004; Baxter et al. 2003); and ICME (Baxter et al. 2004). Mark Baxter (2003) has written independently on his experience of the project. We have also had less formal discussions at local ALM meetings in London. We are grateful to conference and workshop participants, some of whose contributions have been included in our writing (e.g. Baxter et al. 2003).

4.4 Summary

Those were our methods. We chose to undertake a multiple-site descriptive and exploratory case study in order to give a rich description of, and explore issues in, teaching and learning common measures, especially at entry level. Against that background, we used ethnographic research tools to collect our data because these allowed us greater insight into these issues at a level of detail. Throughout the project the research team collected and dealt with the data in a collaborative way, with the teacher researchers taking a full part in both the research aspect of the project (research design, data collection and analysis) and the development aspect (producing and trialling teaching and learning materials). In appendix 4 we discuss our theoretical resources for our views of teaching and learning in mathematics and numeracy, and broader methodological questions relating to teacher research.

5 What is the problem? Identifying the issues

Here we explore issues raised in our research. At the centre are three groups of issues based on classroom and interview data: students' perspectives on the use of measures, and (separately) students' and teachers' perspectives on teaching and learning measures. We conclude by reflecting on the relationship of measures and mathematics. First we describe the limitations and curricular scope of our data.

We researched practice in particular contexts and within the present political, administrative, funding and curricular constraints. All our data is drawn from observations and comments by teachers and students who were, necessarily, working within the ANCC and in particular settings. There were many constraints. The most obvious is the curriculum itself and associated examinations, which constrain teachers' and students' choices. Others include the (necessarily) restricted range of teaching materials and other resources available, the strong focus of staff development on curriculum 'delivery', and patterns of course organisation. Above all, the curriculum and associated funding and management structures, in the places in which we worked, funnelled students and teachers over the term or year towards a narrow goal. It is hard to imagine that a student would have the space during the course to say that all she wanted to work on was, for example, understanding her child's school work, or that if she did express that interest, a teacher would be able to accommodate it. (There are numeracy courses in which students may negotiate individual schemes of work addressing personal goals and unrelated to examination syllabuses, but those were not represented in our project.)

We have not sought to 'cover' the whole measurement curriculum. The *Measures* in the core curriculum are money, length, capacity, weight (mass) and time. We wanted to focus on the aspects of measurement which seemed to us under-researched and which lie within the popular understanding of the meaning of measurement. Hence we decided to exclude money – though it figured often in our discussions of students' understandings of the decimal system.

Length is the first of the common measures to be listed in the curriculum, and in our classroom data it has the strongest representation. Teachers sometimes refer to the derivation of other metric measures from that for length; Liz Richards includes it in her website (http://www.liz.richards.btinternet.co.uk), as do we in the project web pages. We can only speculate about the reasons for the prominence of length. It has the most obvious relationship to number, since rulers can be used as number lines; and there is something about it that makes it the most visible, and perhaps therefore often accessible, of the measures. A length can be directly shown in the page of a book, while a weight may often be described in terms of equivalents ('a bag of sugar') and volume may be illustrated (a picture of a litre of milk, or a cube). In most of the interviews, length, weight and volume all appear, because we asked about them all. Time seemed to researchers and students to be quite different: known (though sometimes not in ways required by the curriculum) and used by everyone in every aspect of their lives. It is discussed below.

In this report we seek to maintain the integrity of the ways in which issues emerged in our data. That has led to us organising it around grounded issues arising from the data, rather than around measures themselves. Thus we coded every reference to length, but we present those discussions in the contexts in which they arose, for example a builder's work.

5.1 The use of measures: students' perspectives

Here we discuss two issues: students' accounts of their existing skills and needs, and their views of the value and use of measurement. We have decided not to separate them: the students themselves link the two and so does the curriculum, through giving a statement of the use and value of numeracy in the opening pages. (The view given in the curriculum will be discussed in section 8.)

First, Lambeth College numeracy students, in a discussion with their Communications teacher Joe Bangs, introduce key themes:

Joe   *What if measurement wasn't taught? [...]*

George   *If measurement wasn't taught, just do it, measure your own way out.*

Enid   *Measurement wasn't taught when they built the pyramids. [...] They are perfect! If you look at the picture of the pyramids, all up equal sides and it's a triangle or something like that [...]*

Joe   *So they must have developed some kind of skill.*

Enid   *Skill anyway. [...]*

George   *Yeah, there must be some sort of system that they do.*

Enid   *Along the line – [we] used to use string to measure the road, roadworks.*

George   *But it was some sort of measurement.*

Enid   *Measure a car along the line.*

George   *You would measure a car, and say – that's a yard – or a yardstick that I used to see my granddad use to measure the road. [...] They used a footstep to measure as well.*

Winnie   *Did that get taught them?*

George   *It was just something that they worked out [...] OK, measure my foot, whatever, one, two, three, four.*

Enid   *A certain size.*

George   *They just make a step and [...] measure the amount of steps. [...] I think as time goes by knowledge increased, and maybe people started doing a wider range of work, more building, and tried to be more professional. And people tried to learn more, in the classroom which we do the theory, but we also have to do the practical, because I've seen people come to my workplace with the theory, oh, they have all these papers, but they couldn't do the work. [Others laughing.] So they have to learn from you that's there, which maybe don't have the papers. [...] Because they have an idea, they have the this, they*

have the that, but to put it together, maybe they can't do it, but they have it in
paper, they could read it. But they can't do it. So they have to maybe learn
from you, and watch what you are doing, even if they have the paper maybe,
look back on the paper and watch what you do. They both work together.

The ancient Egyptians had both a system of common measures and mathematics education (Fauvel & Gray, 1987; Joseph, 1991; Lumpkin, 1997), but it is likely that their highly educated designers also had to collaborate with skilled workers. The discussion touches on questions raised throughout the project: informal measures are often adequate; you can invent them ('measure your own way out', 'a certain size'); people collaborate to share (or buy in) skills and achieve tasks; measures are rooted in social history; and technological change goes hand in hand with developments in measurement techniques. We turn now to students' views of measurement, in three broad groups.

5.1.1 'If you cannot pass this one, how can you move up?'

The largest single group of the students we have interviewed are not interested in working on measurement for their own immediate use, but because it is included in examinations, and/or they want to help their children:

> *With me it's in case my child comes home, and helping her. I know it, so I can show*
> *her. (Priscilla)*

> *I know how to judge my food [...] so you don't need to measure anything. [...] I'll do*
> *[measurement], but I'm just not interested in it. [...] It's not anything to do with working,*
> *me getting a job or anything, it's not going to have nothing to do with that side of things*
> *anyway. (Ann)*

Work on measures is required for exams, and therefore for further educational progress:

> *For me and many students who are going up to university level, [...] they want to test*
> *you and see if you have passed all this stuff, to get higher. If you cannot pass this one*
> *how can you move up? How can you move higher? (Rose)*

Bob gamely worked on measures because it was part of the package he had signed up for:

> *I think [measurement] needs to be done because it's part of the course. [...] It needs to*
> *be covered, I'm covering it. [The interviewer, Alison Tomlin, asked if it fitted with other*
> *numeracy work:] It seems quite separate. [...] You're doing bits and pieces of things*
> *which aren't connected up because it's all part of the course you know, part of the*
> *year's plan. (Bob)*

The teacher-researchers shared Bob's view that measures were not 'connected up'. The scheme of work and teaching ideas discussed in the next section were in part developed in order to address this problem.

Some HMP Brixton men argued against bothering with measures in the numeracy classroom at all. They laughed at the idea: one said 'You don't carry a tape measure to a shop.' Alison asked about other measures, but they dismissed them:

> *Dutch: They should put the emphasis on what we need to survive on a day-to-day*

basis. Algebra, decimals, fractions – if you leave here and you want business
or you have an interview, they give you a maths test.

Peter: *It makes your cv look better, doesn't it.*

Dutch: *You get interested people come to classes.*

'Surviving' requires mathematics, not for its direct applications, but because some level of
mathematics qualification is required for many jobs. Dutch's 'interested' people were those
with enquiring minds; and those people, Dutch believed, do not want work on measures.
Nevertheless, to improve their cvs they will have to work on them.

Elizabeth said she used a combination of maps and a milometer to find and measure
distances on cycling holidays, but didn't find any practical value in one of her classes on
length and capacity:

> *We went over painting a room [in a class with Mark Baxter], the area of a wall and then*
> *working out how many pots of paint you'd need, but in reality you just get some paint*
> *and if it runs out you go to Homebase and get some more. I wouldn't personally bother*
> *measuring the area of the wall, and then converting it into how many litres […] But I*
> *can see how a painter and decorator would, to cut down his costs, because he'd have*
> *less wastage.*

She points us to the second group of students: those who see measurement as a vital skill.

5.1.2 'It's a basic thing – it's to do with being informed'

When we talked, at Belmarsh, about many students seeing no practical need to work on
measures, Matthew commented:

> *Some people don't bother to read a newspaper. […] It's a basic thing – […] it's to do with*
> *being informed.*

The students who argued that it was important to include measures in mathematics courses
were often people whose working lives required skills in particular aspects of measurement:

> *My trade is decorating, so I need to know litres and measurements and how much a*
> *litre is going to take. Definitely for decorating.* (Malcolm)

Malcolm had gained those skills while combining work with a day-release course. By the time
he joined Eamonn Leddy's course, therefore, he already had the measurement skills he
needed.

Whiteley (Belmarsh) described working as a builder on garden swimming pools. He drew a
sketch to explain to Alison what he was talking about, but said he was no good at 'writing it
down and explaining' (a sketch evidently did not count as 'writing it down'). He described
himself as 'OK at diagrams but not in mathematical terms'. Prior to starting work, he would
make a portfolio of pictures showing the job at every stage: 'skims, returns, drains,
underwater lights, triangle braces, concrete ring beams – where they all are, how they fit.' To
make a sloping swimming pool, he measured the length and width, and 'squared it in' (i.e.
made it rectangular) by measuring the diagonals. To get the slope right, he would first dig

down and use a vertical measure to check depth: 'Then you hope the man working the digger is good at his job and he'll make an even, flat slope.' If not, Whiteley checked, using string.

Checking something is 'square' by using diagonals is a technique in many cultures and mathematical systems (see, for example, Gerdes, 1997), and is highly practical, requiring no equipment other than string. Whiteley's skills are beyond those required at entry level 3 – or perhaps they are just in a different world.

Simon Bridge, a carpet layer, gave this estimate of the area of a circle:

> *You square it off from the widest point. It's about seven-eighths of the total area. No, four-fifths, round about 80 per cent.*

(The class, working with Topo Wresniwiro, checked this estimate and found it to be remarkably close to that given by using the standard formula.) Here again a student described a method that is not required in the curriculum – and if it were, it would be above entry level 3.

Two students, both skilled in the use of imperial measures, highly valued their classroom work on metric measures and saw it as directly relevant to life outside the classroom. Paul works in the food industry. His initial reason for taking up courses was to improve his literacy, 'But now coming back to [Lambeth] College I realise that mathematics is as important as literacy.'

> *I'm always working in the food industry where I have to weigh [...] and maybe write it down as well, for inspection. [...] But as the years go by, and working in the food industry, [...] I found it was getting harder and harder for me. [...] I was brought up with pounds and ounces, so that's what I know. [...] Really if I do [cooking] at home, or sometimes when I do it at work, sometimes I don't bother weighing. Because I've been doing it for a long time. It's just knowing the right amount to put in. Maybe that's not the best way, because the employer needs to know the amount that you put in to make up a recipe. To him it is important. To me maybe it's not, because I am just doing, and I know what I'm doing. But they want to know what I'm doing.*

Paul describes the need to cross the gap between his own skills and those needed by employers and inspectors as his industry changes. Geraldine (Westminster Kingsway) similarly found her world changing with the introduction of the metric system. A seamstress and a single mother looking to economise where possible, she valued new learning in metric measurement as a way to save money and prevent shopkeepers cheating her:

> *When I went to buy material to do my work, the man behind the counter was using a yard stick on metre measurements. I said, 'What are you doing?' He said, 'I'm just using my finger to give you a little bit more'. And I said: 'You are supposed to use the right measurement [...] You are cheating me.' And so I'm [in the classes] for them to teach me – if they don't, people easily can rob you. If I know, I can shout out and say: 'You are cheating the people in the shop'. [...] I apply [what I learn in the class] when I go out, anytime.*

Paul and Geraldine were already skilled in the imperial measurements they needed, but wanted to be equally confident in the metric system. In seeing classroom measurement work as combining immediate practical benefits with educational progression, they represent the kind of student we believe the government has in mind. However, they are in a minority in so neatly fitting the government model. We note too that both initially sought literacy rather than numeracy education; even for Paul and Geraldine, improving their skills in measures was not their primary aim in returning to education.

Most students then fell into two broad groups: those who do not use 'common' measures and those who see measurement as a vital, practical skill. The latter group have the skills they need (often developed through work, rather than in formal education), at least in some measures, and find it hard to imagine the world without them; the former do not need the skills. Even those who argue for the importance of measurement probably do not use what they learn in the classroom, but rather what they have learned outside. None, though, has said that measurement should not be included in the syllabus. Because it is in the school and adult numeracy curricula, it is essential for helping children and for examinations.

The students quoted above see measures in specific contexts, whether that be a test, or selling carpets, or meeting a supervisor's standards. We turn now to a different route to thinking about measures: as central to mathematics and to communication.

5.1.3 'To communicate with people, you do need measurement.'
We argued above that measures are a foundation stone of mathematics. When Topo asked Fergus about measurement he replied in terms of mathematics. Topo checked ('So you think measurement is an important topic?'), and Fergus continued:

> Yes, in truth. Because it's not only measurement in terms of a length. It's measurement in terms of – if you have a pound, what do you do with it? You invest it and I think measurement, by the actual sound of the word measurement, you have a conceived idea already. [...] So in terms of the whole of mathematics, I think it's one of the fundamentals of society in general, that without it you are lacking in a lot of aspects that would benefit your life.

Our focus in this project excluded money, but it is a measure; Fergus drew attention to the function of measures in social exchange generally.

We quoted Elizabeth above, saying she had no need for measures relating to decorating. However, towards the end of her conversation with June (another student) and Alison, she changed her view. June introduced the idea of measures as helping communication:

I like to learn actually, about all these measurements [...] Just to be more aware of this measurement and how it works. How would you be able to [say] the measurement to the others?

Elizabeth commented:

> I didn't come on this course to understand measurement. I came on this course to get all of my fundamental maths skills together. [...] Whilst we are talking about measurement I've realised that I do, actually, want to know about it. Because I do think it helps you understand. [...] Well, I think, in order to communicate with people I think you've got to have the same language. For example, in miles, you know, you were saying how many miles and if somebody says – oh it's a five-minute walk – like you

[Alison] said, that's not standardised, because someone's five minutes might be somebody else's three minutes or somebody else's ten minutes. So distance is a black and white, it is as it is. It's not a variable. So I think you do, to communicate with people, you do need measurement.

We started this discussion of students' views of the meanings of measures with students talking about ancient Egypt, and we finish with a vague but expansive and suggestive view of measures as a part of human culture and language. The project website, www.nrdc.org/measures will include an article on an Egyptian measurement of the circumference of the world, as we attempt to offer some routes into the cultural and historical place of measures. In section 6 we discuss work on measures which, we argue, addresses some of the students' implied criticisms of our usual ways of teaching.

5.2 Teaching and learning: students' perspectives

We turn now to students' views of their courses. We saw above that they did not agree on the purposes or value of studying measures; in contrast, their comments on courses, teachers and learning were remarkably consistent. Much of our discussion here is not directly about measures, but about learning and teaching numeracy more generally: the classroom contexts for work on measures.

5.2.1 'Communicating very well': classroom relationships

Although some students had criticisms of the pace of courses (below), and by implication the scheme of work, none criticised the teaching. There is, always, a problem in researching adult students' views of teaching: very often, if a teacher is, in the student's view, failing them, the student leaves, so we are usually dealing with a group who are self-selected as (more or less) content with the teaching. When we asked about teaching, students focused on their perceptions of the teacher's attitude to and relationship with the students. We need to be cautious: students were not likely to risk undermining their relationship with their teacher, and there is some evidence that students speak more critically to each other than to their teacher (Tomlin, 2001). The only students who decided against being interviewed were Liz's 16–18 group; they are also the only group whose motivation for attending was unclear. Given these cautions, one theme emerged very clearly.

Above all, good teachers are seen as caring about the students (cf. Gardener (1992), on the teaching of writing):

[Mark] has to leave his base almost every day. It's his good will to give us things to do. ... In this prison you have good teachers, great teachers, but in this prison they have to be hunting us down to find us. (Dutch)

Why [Eamonn] really motivates me and I really look up to him, he was the one who actually said I should go for the accountancy ... He said – go, do it. He gave me the motivation to go and do it. (Geraldine)

Students who have two teachers agree their teaching is different, but these Lambeth students value both:

Carl: *Liz have her own feel in maths, Victoria have her own feel in maths.*

> *Ann: They teach differently.*

> *Carl: Maybe I understand more with Liz. Other people would understand more with Victoria.*

Appreciation of the teacher leads to generalising from their practice:

> *I think you should follow Eamonn's example and give a lot of worksheets to practise and check with each student if they understand and made sure they understand by calling them to answer, each one of them, any questions.* (Emma)

In analysing why they trust the teacher, some students discussed the greater confidence that they felt as a result of being known individually, in sharp contrast to school and some previous adult education experiences. Though several FE students mentioned this, it was particularly important in the two prisons:

> *[The benefit] was also that I could relate to you [Topo] on a one to one.[...] And I'm allowed to make my own mistakes. It's not a daunting prospect of saying to you – Teach, I'm now stuck. When I came in here [HMP Belmarsh], I was – oh my chest has got to be higher, I've got to more or less be the bad boy, yeah? Which that entails, basically, nobody's got to talk to you because you didn't owe nobody nothing. [...] Because a lot of us in here, because of the environment we run as a pack and not as an individual. Because in here it's like, you've got to be continuously showing out.* (Fergus)

As we have described, the FE college classes were based around group work on a common topic, while the prisons offered largely individual work. It may be here simply that students praise their own teachers' approaches, but we think that's unlikely. Prisoners describe the classrooms as a comparatively safe haven where 'face' is less at risk.

FE students valued individual relationships with their teachers, but also group work, allowing supportive relationships among the students themselves. Here Rose links the two:

> *You understand what I mean, working as a team? I can work on my own. She can work on her own, [he] can work on [his] own, everybody can work on their own, that's what is brilliant here [Westminster Kingsway College]. We are all working to learn. But the only thing I mean is this: I am doing my own, so you don't know what I am doing. But working as a team we all know that we are doing this task. Everybody got their own task. Are you getting on well? That's what I mean, by working as team members, you know how to communicate with people, when you go out you can communicate very well.*

'Communicating very well' is the point, for prison and FE students alike, and it is a point more often made about language and literacy than numeracy classes. Good teachers (in students' view, but we agree) foster classroom cultures which support trust and open communication.

Students' comments on what makes a good teacher carry implied judgements of teaching they have experienced in the past (both at school and as an adult). Several explicitly contrasted their present teacher with stories of humiliation or lost, wasted time in previous classes, with teachers who didn't care (as far as the students could see) about teaching or the students. Those are not quoted here, but they strengthen the case for the centrality of the teacher-student personal relationship. Students seek respect from their teacher and from each other.

5.2.2 'Bringing your ideas to your friends': mutual support

One apparent difference between the FE classrooms was the seating arrangement: in Lambeth, students sat behind tables in a horseshoe arrangement, facing the board; in Westminster Kingsway, they sat in small groups at separate tables (known as a 'café' or 'cabaret' layout). Alison asked some of the students about this. They all argued their own was best:

> *If it was more like that [separate tables] I would feel less likely to ask the others. Because, you see, this [horseshoe] is one, everybody is all joined. We are connected. Whereas if you go to a restaurant when everybody is at their own table and you get that feeling that you are in your own space – so it's harder to talk with other people.*
> (Foxtrot, a Lambeth student commenting on the café arrangement)

Westminster Kingsway students argued for the 'café' arrangement:

> *Priscilla*   *At this table I concentrate better. I am used to this place and when I'm here I feel good and comfortable and I understand what my teacher is saying. If I move I am likely to be distracted.*
>
> *Emma*   *This table is our table.*
>
> *Andrea*   *And we know this is our table.*

Both groups answered a question about room layout with comments about relationships of mutual support within the group. We understood that despite the institutional feel of FE colleges, the students had in common a sense of ownership of shared space: 'this is our table', 'everybody is all joined'.

Foxtrot and Hotel (Lambeth College) argued for class time without a teacher. They were the only two who advocated this, but we include their proposal because it is consistent with others' requests for more time and their generally collaborative ways of working. One day a teacher was absent, but sent work for the group:

> *Hotel*   *Yeah, it was like teaching one another and we came back with very good answers […] Students should be able to share ideas. […] When somebody was asking a question, you know what to say, you know, to teach your friends. It is very important. But if a teacher continues teaching …*
>
> *Foxtrot*   *More, before you've learnt.*
>
> *Hotel*   *… the next day you should be given half an hour, at one another, in bringing your ideas to your friends and then they can look into it.*
>
> *Alison*   *[…] But do you find that if you are asking another student a question that the student understands your question easier than a teacher [does]?*
>
> *Foxtrot*   *Oh man.*

Hotel   *Sometimes.*

Foxtrot   *Because you've got that thing that's not there. You know? When you see a teacher you see authority.[...] But when you are dealing with another student who is on the same level as you, you are there to learn, they are there to learn.*

5.2.3 'You need a teacher to tell you': measuring progress

Measuring something is a practical skill, but when we asked students how they knew if they were making progress few referred to the application of new skills beyond the classroom. Geraldine (whom we described above as seeing real practical relevance in classroom work) said she knew she was making progress both because she had metric measures 'in her head' for use in the shopping, and had done classroom work correctly:

It's more I can go out and apply it and see the measurement in my head and know that they are not cheating me on that measurement. And to look at my file and say, 'Yeah, I achieved this.'

Most students identified their progress through correct classroom work, or passing tests:

It's not just like a feeling. You need a teacher to tell you. [...] I might as well have not gone to college if I think I can do it all by myself. (Foxtrot)

Because in our assessment I've been doing well, maybe 30 questions I will get like 26, 27. So I know I'm improving. (Hotel)

I think I'm doing well, [...] because I was doing the same course last year, and I was really left behind. [...] But this year I'm going forward quite easy. (Bob)

[Eamonn] mixes the questions up [...] and he gives old test papers. You've done this already, so why should you get it wrong? But it's good how he does it. (Emma)

It's a closed world: study measures because they are in the curriculum, then measure progress against the curriculum. The society outside, where everything is measured, might as well not exist.

5.2.4 'We haven't got time to make it register': pace, learning and recalling

Here students' views are so similar to teachers' that we put them together, starting with the students'. When a Lambeth group discussed the shape of their course they focused on the question of the pace of study – or perhaps the pace of learning, since their concern was that there was too little time to absorb new ideas. The course had two teachers. Liz (in the case discussed here) introduced new topics, and the other followed it up but with, in the students' view, too long a gap and too little time overall. The criticism was not of the teachers, but of the course design:

Sharon   *Some teachers, you are dying to understand it – they are jumping to something else. [...] They are telling us it's the syllabus, we are behind, or something. ..Some people can pick things fast, some of us, like myself, are very slow. [...] If we do this leaflet today......*

> Ann   Yes, I know what she's going to say.

> Sharon   .... when we finish this today, tomorrow – we don't go over it again.

> Ann   We do something else.[...] It doesn't stay in, because she is saying we move on to something else every week, which is true.

> Alison   So you think you need a longer -

> Sharon   Not longer, maybe I understand it this week. Maybe the next person don't understand. Sometimes I do, but sometimes I don't. And the following day we haven't even finished this, we are on something else.

> Ann   I'm worried about the exams because I feel the same way. We don't spend long enough on the same thing. [...] Yeah, I have forgotten what we learned at the beginning of the course.

Westminster Kingsway students, on a course with one tutor, agreed:

> We are moving too fast, you know? [...] We haven't got time to make it register. [...] We've got to get on to something else. And well, with me, anyway, I'm not that fast. (Malcolm)

For the teacher-researchers too there was not enough time. Teachers and students are not convinced that the new skills and knowledge are 'sinking in' – becoming part of common sense perhaps, available for ever.

> I enjoyed (and I think the students did too) the discussion part of all this, but it didn't leave us enough time for the 'practical' exercises, and most of it was surplus to minimum curriculum requirements. (Eamonn)

The scare quotes round 'practical' point to the fact that measurement so often feels impractical because it is driven by the syllabus rather than by student curiosity or need. 'It's the syllabus, we are behind', said Sharon, catching the demands on teachers to 'deliver' the curriculum.

In our present policy contexts there is little discussion about the meanings of remembering and learning, and the question is unlikely to be unique to work on measurement, or indeed to numeracy. The three-part lesson promoted through the *Skills for Life* three-day training (DfES & Basic Skills Agency, 2001b) proposes that previous learning be reviewed in the first part of the lesson, and it is assumed that will 'work'. But if it doesn't – if students are still not confident – the demand that students 'achieve' by the end of the course leads to the feeling that all are riding an unstoppable train:

> Some are now answering with the perimeter when I ask them the area of the shape; it's on to volume next. (Liz, class notes)

The teacher-researchers used common techniques for checking understanding (including questioning, mini-tests and asking students to review their progress). Those techniques are felt to be inadequate when teaching is so pressured:

I think they did learn or at least re-recall the names of the measurements in the metric system and the relationship between cm and mm. (Liz, class notes)

Here Liz does not know whether this is new or revived old knowledge. If the students already 'knew' the relationship between cm and mm, they didn't know it in an immediately accessible way – and that almost certainly means that they do not use them. The fact that many students don't use standard measures in outside-class life makes the study of measurement an abstract endeavour. Each of the teacher-researchers had 'practical' work – real measuring – at the heart of their lesson planning, but nevertheless students were trying to learn new facts and skills just in the time available in the class. Numbers are everywhere, but 'common' measures, for many, are only in the classroom.

The pace in the prisons was quite different. In both, most work was individually planned; compared to FE, students could have twice the time (per week) for numeracy; each lesson was longer; and there was less sense of a deadline because examinations were available very frequently (in order to cope with the high turnover). We have noted however that students in Belmarsh working at entry level 3 seemed more advanced than those in FE, and that at least one Brixton prisoner (Ade) was taking tests at an inappropriately low level. It may be therefore that the prison students were not, in some cases, being asked to learn as much new material as those in FE.

5.3 Teaching and learning measures: teachers' perspectives

Turning to teachers' perspectives, we draw out issues developed through discussions in the research team meetings and data analysis; some come directly from the project, while others have haunted the teachers for years but are illustrated with project data.

5.3.1 Proxies: 10 minutes' walk, light years and ratios

Familiar or informal measures can be used as proxies for others. Distance is often expressed as time to travel. Students at HMP Brixton described to Mark how to find small weights of drugs by repeated splitting into tenths, judged by eye rather than direct weighing; Mark noticed that in a parallel move, he broke matchsticks (using lengths judged by eye) to demonstrate small weights. These uses of proxies seem to be typical of people's use of non-standard measurements, and consistent with our general finding that 'common' measures are often unnecessary. We have seen above that Elizabeth changed her mind about the value of common measures in discussion of the difficulties caused, in some circumstances, by the (often) non-standard nature of such proxies – but the proxies are extraordinarily useful.

Walking speeds may vary, but '10 minutes' walk' is more informative than 'a kilometre' to many of us. Scientific discourse too has a proxy, in this case a standard measure: the light year, again using time to measure distance. Proxies point us to our purposes for measuring. Measures are rarely needed singly. Laying carpet, getting to an appointment, buying petrol or cooking lentils need respectively width and length, time and distance, volume and money, and volume or weight (lentils), volume (water) and time. 'Dealing' with them (that is, both using or understanding the measures, and organising social exchange) is complex. Rendering the measures discrete, in order to teach them, takes them out of the contexts in which people handle them every day.

5.3.2 Decimal numbers

Metric measures are based on a decimal system, and much of the curriculum (and more of the tests) is concerned with conversions: 1200 g to 1.2 kg, 0.5 l to 500 ml, and so on.

To understand the size of a number, you must understand place value based on powers of 10 (the 3 in 300 is 3×10^2). It hasn't always been so, and some non-decimal numbers are still in use ('three score years and ten' in the Bible; a dozen eggs) – but base 10 is now so naturalised that its structure is invisible unless you are teaching or learning it. Many teaching approaches seek to use the whole numbers to explain decimals ('as you go to the right the numbers carry on getting 10 times smaller'). The metric system of measures was designed to be rational and internally consistent, in contrast to earlier piecemeal, local and ill-fitting systems. Metric measures are based on the decimal number system we all know, so things should be straightforward – but they are not, as we illustrate here.

> *Andrea measured the door and wrote 1.80 cm. I said to her that that looked as though it was less than 2 cm, and she could put either 1.8 m or 1 m 80 cm. She looked very doubtful […]. She definitely knew what she meant. Eamonn came over and reminded her of earlier work on money and she accepted his explanation. This would probably not be a problem for Andrea in most 'real life' contexts; she knew perfectly well she had used a whole metre and 80 cm more; a DIY shop wouldn't accept at face value an instruction to cut wood to 1.80 cm.* (Alison's notes)

Andrea 'knew what she meant': she knew which measures (a whole metre and more) she had used; the difficulty was in the units and decimals.

Conversions between metric measure units (centimetres to metres, etc.) depend on multiplying and dividing by powers of 10. Many students used the 'standard' multiplication algorithm, laying out the numbers in columns; all the teachers thought it important that students learn to use the decimal place value structure, moving numbers to left or right in relation to the decimal point. We illustrate this with episodes from three classrooms.

Geraldine (Westminster Kingsway) was converting 9.9 cm to millimetres and said hesitantly, 'Nine hundred and -', then paused. Meanwhile others were discussing it, and someone said it was 99. Geraldine queried it: 'I thought you put the zero down?' (a reference to the column layout).

$$9.9$$
$$\times 10$$
$$99.0$$

Eamonn wrote out the column layout on the board, getting 990 and writing in the decimal point (99.0): 'You have *one* number after the decimal point because there's one up here' (in 9.9) and adding, 'But you don't *need* to do that, you can just move the decimal point.'

Liz (Lambeth) said of one class, when students kept saying they wanted the method they knew (the vertical layout algorithm), 'I gave up':

> *My theory is that a considerable amount of time spent on learning techniques/rules by students would be done away with if they had a good understanding of the number system they are working in. […] I think students cannot understand why they need to learn another technique for a limited range of calculations which they can do perfectly well in the traditional way. I'm beginning to wonder if perhaps we should go along with this, still continually (referring to the short way but letting them come to it when they are ready.*

Elizabeth and June (South Thames College) discussed changing whole kilometres to metres. In one question, Elizabeth had added two zeros instead of three. These two students reverse the picture given in the two accounts above: Elizabeth was used to moving figures in relation to the decimal point, but thought it a dangerous practice, while June, used to the column layout, had done as Mark (and Eamonn, in the example above) advised and moved the decimal point. As they went over the problem, June (who had herself added zeros) wrote out the column layout calculation to explain to Elizabeth why three zeros were needed. Elizabeth criticised herself for moving the point:

> Elizabeth   *You didn't have to understand [the mathematics] to do it. Well, I didn't – you can just add zeros and things. [...] You just move the decimal point, and that's when I made a mistake.*

> June   *I prefer it this way, the longer way.*

> Elizabeth   *I can see why, because you understand how you get to the solution. Whereas with this you are like – OK, I'm just moving a point along because I've been told to.*

> June   *It might be more confusing.*

> Elizabeth   *Whereas here [in the column layout] you can see the process. That's how I see it.*

'You can see the process': what did Elizabeth mean? Some students refer to moving the decimal point as 'cheating', as though it is cutting corners, and that is perhaps what Elizabeth was getting at. Certainly in the column layout you can see *more* process – it takes more time and paper – but if anything it obscures the structure of the decimal system.

We turn back now to the relationship of metric measures with the decimal system. We have said that metric measures were designed to fit with decimal numbers. If we take a longer and wider view, there is an argument for reversing the order: fractional numbers, including decimals, were developed in order to measure things. This was first put to us by Margaret Brown (King's College London) as we discussed our concerns with decimal numbers, but Kamar, in an entry level 3 class (seeking to improve her English for mathematics) but a mathematics graduate, made the same point:

> *Mathematics is [...] very important to know, because it is important for our life. [...] When you measure your height or you want to weigh yourself, and it's very important to know the scales, how they divide themselves. Because they don't come exactly the number.*

'They don't come exactly the number': you are unlikely to weigh exactly, say, 68 kg. But the gram, rather than kilogram, is the basic unit of metric measures of weight: in saying 'kilo' we are already multiplying by 1,000. The system is designed to avoid hard-to-manage numbers, whether large or small:

> *Where you're trying to get higher and higher gradations, you're driven into decimals, though people avoid decimals by creating smaller and smaller units, so there's a sense in which you can almost avoid decimals completely. The problem is that you invent [the*

units system – mg/g/kg, etc.] to get rid of these things [decimals], and then when
you're calculating it's a lot better to get rid of all the units and just use one. So the
advantages and disadvantages of both are worth talking about, but nobody ever does.
(Margaret Brown, discussion)

And what of using money as a springboard for understanding decimals? We have said that
Andrea, in difficulties with decimal numbers and units of length, was reminded by Eamonn of
their work on money. The class had discussed why £1.68 is correct, and £1.68p is not (the unit
is pounds). All the team have experience, however, of money not being an adequate lead-in to
understanding decimals:

It's too much of a separate unit ... basically you have pence and you have pounds, and
there's no need ever to get into a decimal, unless you want to do rapid calculations on a
calculator, in which case it becomes convenient to count your pence as decimals of a
pound. You don't actually have to understand it at all. (Margaret Brown, discussion)

It should not be surprising that we haven't an 'answer' here, but we found a way forward for
our own teaching and research practice. The measures encountered in examinations are very
often either conversions or calculations, driving us to work on arithmetic:

In the flurry to get men through examinations I was teaching even less measure. How
much measure is there in level 1 and 2 examinations? Not much and it is of an abstract
nature. Is measure just about converting between units? (Mark)

We decided to focus instead on the processes of *measuring* – an activity – so that any
calculations are necessary and integral to the measuring, rather than the whole point.

5.3.3 Time: 'You don't need to add up and think'

When you look at your watch you don't need to add up and think – oh that's time. [...]
Say the bus is coming at twenty past and it was a five-minute walk from your house,
you'd look at your watch and think – oh it's quarter past, I can make it in time if I leave
now. That's common knowledge, isn't it? (Mark, HMP Belmarsh)

No students or tutors have commented on having difficulties with the teaching or learning of
the measurement of time. There are gaps in knowledge: for example, some students do not
know the number of days of months and some have some difficulty with reading calendars of
different layouts. But whereas metric measures are unfamiliar to many, the basic units of
time – seconds, hours, weeks, years and so on – are well known and used. Similarly, while
some students may have problems using rulers, no-one has reported having difficulties with
clocks or watches (setting the video has been mentioned as a problem, but it is unclear
whether the difficulty is with time or other elements of the process). No-one has reported
having difficulty telling the time or timing events (though that may not translate into solving
word problems on time or using the 24-hour clock); some students are unsure of the 'rarities'
of time, for example leap years or working backwards to find a date. Unlike other standard
measures, adults have commonly to manage their time, including managing their children's.
(We recognise that some people do have difficulty telling and managing time, but at the
curriculum levels at which we worked, broadly entry 2 to level 1, they were not represented.)

Time also has more associations with cultural, creative and religious life than have other
measures. Following classes which variously included discussion of '9/11' compared to

'September 11th' (2001), Islamic, Jewish and Christian calendars, calculating birthdays and days of the week, and astrology, Eamonn and Liz commented on the gap between the classroom discussion and the demands of the curriculum. Eamonn (quoted above) noted that the discussion was enjoyable but did not leave time for 'practical' exercises; Liz commented:

> *They enjoyed the lesson [...] though it was probably more valuable for general knowledge than numeracy.*

Eamonn's 'practical' exercises were completing worksheets on time – the sorts of worksheets which prepare students for tests. His inverted commas indicate his caution about their practicality. Liz commented on a lesson on time:

> *This seems to have been a session beset by worksheets, which given the inherent practical nature of time worries me somewhat.*

These then may be examples of students' interests and teachers' willingness to accommodate them being restrained by the curriculum. Students and teacher-researchers seem to enjoy working on time: they are able to work playfully with it, driven by curiosity rather than by the required curriculum.

Measures are arbitrary, but the metric system was designed to be rational - to fit together. Some units of time (at least on the surface) make no sense: there is no intrinsic reason for there to be 24 hours in a day or seven days in a week, for example. The units are only patchily internally consistent. 60 seconds, 60 minutes and 360 degrees in a circle are all inherited from Babylonian mathematics (a system which, based on 60, had a parallel internal consistency to that of the decimal/metric systems) but seven days in a week do not neatly fit with the days in a calendar month, though they do fit with a lunar month of 28 days.

The system of units for measuring time has not changed in centuries; French republicans invented a base 10 system of time (having, for example, a 10 day 'week') but it was soon abandoned (Hebra, 2003). There could be an argument then that this is why the units of measurement of time are more familiar: they have not been subjected to our comparatively recent switch to the metric system. But we are told that numeracy students in countries where the metric system has been established for over 100 years also have difficulties with it. Comparative familiarity with the measurement of time must then come from its persistent utility and necessity in our society; unlike some other measures, it is not disappearing from everyday life.

We have said that adults have to manage 'their' time; we also say: 'I haven't got time', 'I wasted time', 'I'll make time', 'I killed time', 'I lost track of time'. It has a life of its own: 'time stood still', 'I don't know where the time's gone', and 'the years passed quickly'. Time is profoundly personal, imagined, felt, controlled and controlling (cf. Mace, 1998). 'What is the time?' the root question in the time curriculum, does not come near our skills, knowledge and emotional relationships with time.

5.3.4 'Almost no written work to show for this lesson': discussion as a learning approach

We have quoted students praising their classroom seating arrangements in terms of the student-student relationships they allow, and proposing student-only time to allow student-initiated conversations. There is a substantial research literature on the value of discussion in mathematics education, much of it developing Vygotskyan perspectives in which learning is seen as an activity in which shared mathematical meanings are constructed socially (Coben et al. 2003). The meanings of 'discussion' are themselves much discussed in mathematics education research; in an article presenting five researchers debating among themselves the place and value of conversation in mathematics classrooms, Anna Sfard concludes:

> *Perhaps all one can say right now is that for a conversation to be productive, it has to have the characteristics of a true dialogue.* (Sfard et al. 1998, p.51)

It is difficult to have a 'true dialogue' in adult numeracy classrooms working to the national numeracy curriculum. Those organised around individual work may, surprisingly, come close, since it is possible that if students choose to collaborate they are 'left alone' enough in the overall patterns of classroom discourse to develop their own conversation. That demands that the teacher adopt particular stances: not silencing, however accidentally or subtly, conversations which may appear to be 'off task'; not interrupting in an effort to be helpful; perhaps not listening in, so that space is left for 'wrong' ideas to be explored. However successful this permissive, rather than directive, approach to conversation, it is possible that some students will remain in a world whose discursive horizons are hemmed in by the worksheet or textbook, the teacher, and their own past histories and experiences of mathematics education.

Individual work in the numeracy classroom is still, we believe, a widely adopted model, and Belmarsh and Brixton students had individual work. On the other hand, the lesson structure promoted in official discourses (DfES & Basic Skills Agency, 2001b) includes the whole-class work, teacher-led discussion and small group work of the FE teacher-researchers in our study. There is, however, a fixed point to which the discussion must lead, one known by the teacher and not (yet) by the students, since every lesson plan must have a verifiable outcome. Commenting on the introduction of the (schools) national curriculum, Steve Lerman argued that it would lead to a new dependency culture – 'new' in contrast to the shifts in the previous 15 years towards more problem solving and challenges to authority in classrooms adopting constructivist approaches. He then called on teachers to set their own agenda for teaching mathematics in schools and reject the new drift to dependency on outside authorities (Lerman, 1990:159). The ANCC is strongly influenced by the (schools) National Numeracy Strategy, itself a recipe for the delivery of the (schools) national curriculum. Shall we soon have a generation of 'dependent' teachers and students?

We do not think so – we do not feel dependent, but rather steered and controlled. Teacher-researchers' notes record that time spent on discussion is worthwhile:

> *Almost no written work to show for this lesson but I think it did help to put some understanding in place.* (Liz)

Such comments suggest that teachers may feel they have to defend their practice against the idea that discussion is wasting time, not getting through the scheme of work, and so on. This can be read in parallel with Hotel's and Foxtrot's proposal for student-only time to work on mathematics, and students' views that they work best with particular companions. Teachers and learners value discussion, but it is hard to get enough time for it.

The ANCC advocates discussion; we claim that in lessons run according to the ANCC model, there is not enough time for it; meanwhile, Paul Ernest makes the case for conversation as a metaphor for the development of mathematics itself (Ernest, 1998). So discussion and conversation mean different things to different people. We do not pursue that question in this report, but we do argue that the kinds of discussion generated in the work we discuss in the next section are quite different from those envisaged in the ANCC and associated training.

We must however note that some teachers (outside the project) have told us that they value the *Skills for Life* model exactly because it includes discussion. This reminds us that many classrooms where students work individually are not like those in Belmarsh and Brixton prisons: they are quiet, paper-centred, with most talk focused on questions and answers between individuals and the teacher. For some teachers and managers the teaching approaches associated with the curriculum have been liberating.

5.3.5 Measures, size and visual representations

Students' talk when helping each other with worksheets or practical activities often is not apparently about measurement, but about numbers - 'I got 52', for example, rather than 'I think it's 52 centimetres'. When teachers ask students to name the units, they sometimes go through worksheets retrospectively inserting them. The units evidently are not necessary, for many students, to make sense of much of their work on measures. A possible reason for this is that much of it, as we argued above, is not about measuring, but about conversions – that is, calculations. In the next section we discuss some signs of that changing with different, more investigative work, but first we consider the language (vocabulary) of measures and their visual representation.

Geddie chooses to define dimension as:

> *Measure in length, breadth or thickness (the three dimensions of space).* (Geddie, 1964)

The writers of the core curriculum and the national standards define weight (distinguishing it from mass), capacity and volume: the last is 'a measure in three-dimensional space'. However, they do not attempt a definition of terms used for the three dimensions (DfES & Basic Skills Agency, 2001 a:glossary).

The language of dimensions and size is complex and ambiguous. For example, is 'length' always roughly horizontal, or is it the label of the longest dimension? A student from Sierra Leone told us that in his language there is simply no equivalent to the English usage of 'length': one word means 'the longer side' and another means 'the shorter side'. A City and Guilds examination question (available on our website) gives three diagrams of monitors, all cubes, and asks *Which monitor is the narrowest?* For some of us, 'narrow' relates to proportions, that is, it is a relative rather than absolute term – so cubes have the same narrowness. The depth of a swimming pool is in a vertical direction, but a wardrobe's depth is horizontal, and at that, from front to back, not side to side. Mathematics is often described as using language precisely (and sometimes as being itself a language); in English the language of dimensions is absolutely dependent on its discursive context.

The language of dimensions is a rich source for metaphors. 'High' is exposed in some way (high on drugs, high in the organisation); 'deep' is hidden (hidden depths to her character), or profound ('deep down, I don't trust him'). A person may be tall or short, but always has height; a person who is high (up) is either important or standing on a chair; a mountain is rarely tall, but stories may be. 'Thick' goes with 'dense', but someone who is thin is not necessarily sharp. On the other hand, a dense textbook may require deep thinking, and turn out to be shallow. Time may be long or short but not wide, though you may have a high old time on an evening out.

One possibility would be for teachers to fix on a limited group of terms and avoid others, for example using 'wide' and 'width', but not 'broad' and 'breadth', but that could not work: outside the classroom, the ambiguities are real and students have to deal with them. Inside the classroom, students sometimes ask for the one correct word for a particular meaning. Sometimes teachers can provide it, but often there isn't one.

Diagrams are used to amplify meaning and are themselves part of the language of mathematics, but we have examples of diagrams contributing to the blurring of meaning. Eamonn raised for team discussion the wording and illustrations in examination questions (Eamonn's paper is posted on the website). Here is one:

> You want to order a new wardrobe. You log on to the Home Living Site. The space you have is 210 (length) × 90 (width) × 45 (width).

Note the two 'widths'. No units are given and a later question requires students to select appropriate units. There are four 2-D diagrams, drawn nothing like to scale. Not only are they not to the same scale as each other, but the proportions are wrong, so, for example, wardrobe B is labelled '200 × 85 × 40' and is 34 × 29 mm. The 'length' of the question is, presumably, what most people would in this context call height (since width certainly isn't height). One of the questions is: 'which wardrobe is the shortest?' Who can say?

Another question says 'The printer is 50 cm wide and 30 cm long. Circle the box that the printer will fit in.' The boxes are shown in 3-D diagrams (again not in proportion with each other or within each diagram), with only two lengths given (e.g. 70 cm × 20 cm).

The skilful student will work out that the diagrams are not to scale, and will not trust them. That is a mistake with a third question, which shows 'different sizes of envelopes for different things' – though the 'different things' are irrelevant. There are pictures of three envelopes, and this is the question:

> Which is the longest envelope? You will need to measure them.

There is no need to measure: you can see it. The pictures are not really representations – they are themselves the real objects to be compared.

For these questions, wardrobes are drawn in 2-D but have to be dealt with in 3-D; boxes are drawn in 3-D but have to be dealt with in 2-D. The question that asks the student to measure something does so unnecessarily. These diagrams are a top dressing intended to make the paper look more accessible to students, though it is doubtful if they serve that aim.

The questions purport to relate to real-life contexts. Our last example comes from an examination geared to students on construction courses:

> You will need to know the most appropriate unit to use when measuring bricks. Will it be: a) g. b) mm. c) ml. d) kg. (City & Guilds)

The correct answer is b), because builders' measurements of length are usually given in millimetres. But in other circumstances what might be needed is the weight – for example, the maximum load for a lorry, or the weight to be borne by a lintel. The student must judge which context of three possibilities is the most likely.

Examination questions purport to refer to real-life tasks, but the reality has been drained out of them to the point at which, as Ann put it, they are 'not anything to do with working, me getting a job or anything, it's not going to have nothing to do with that side of things'. Our project was not focused on assessment – but both students and teachers are driven in part by the need to achieve the requirements of a testing regime.

Students are required not just to learn new vocabulary, but to be wary of familiar (for first language speakers) meanings while in the classroom yet carry on using them outside. For people less familiar with English the task of understanding the language in which measures are discussed is even more difficult.

5.3.6 Younger students: 'more school, but bleached out completely'

Both Liz and Mark worked with groups of 16 to 18-year-olds, and here we point to some contrasts with adult provision. Liz's notes, working with a 16–18 group, recorded her 'Frustration, desperation, need for strong drink …', and students asking, 'Why is this class so long?' Mark commented on a (different) group of 16 to 18-year-old FE students:

> They have failed to achieve at school. What are they given [at college]? More school, but bleached out completely to the driest of all things in the curriculum, literacy and numeracy. Not just what they failed at school but the utter kernel, deadpan basic skills. And they must have heard that word 'basic' so many times used as an insult … Most have failed to get onto a vocational course … None of their basic skills courses relates to vocational training. All core-curriculum based.

> No concentration. No interest in work. Very easily distracted as if it's the norm. In the situation as it is less than half are going to get this qualification. They don't learn anything and the college isn't helped in getting its targets, so what's the point? One student had said he wanted to do electrical engineering and was told by a tutor that he would need to do a lot of maths. He does the bare minimum. Didn't get the point? Bored? Easily done when the work doesn't relate to engineering.

Mark here points to the gap between one student's motivation and context and the course to which he had been directed. The 'targets' are the college's targets for numbers of students gaining qualifications, one of the means through which the success of government policy is measured. Mark then is arguing here both that the student is not achieving his own aims, and the course is not contributing to the government's achievement of its national targets.

The students did not want to be interviewed, so we have only teachers' perceptions of the students' apparent disengagement from their courses. These younger students were doing courses which covered much the same material as the adult courses, where the teachers' work was praised by the students; we assume the 'bleached out' effect comes in part from the very different relationships between students and tutors, and therefore different classroom discourse. The students received the educational maintenance allowance (EMA), which encouraged them to come to college and may be their main 'motivation' for attending. We have discussed our concerns with teachers (outside the project) who described the enthusiastic engagement of groups of 16 to 18-year-olds: perhaps relationships depend on the particular students and teachers; perhaps other colleges have a wider range of courses and choice for students – and so on. Our comments here are necessarily speculative, but we must record that for some young people, in some classrooms, the ANCC simply is not working.

Further, we must raise questions about what will happen if, in response to government measures to meet the *Skills for Life* achievement targets, people enrol on courses for which they have little enthusiasm and of which they cannot see the point. In section 8 we discuss questions for policy raised through the project's work.

5.3.7 'Smaller and smaller units of time': teachers' working lives

Here we put the teaching of measures into the wider context of teachers' working lives. Liz recorded her frustration with a college's change of tack, involving late changes to accreditation policies and therefore additional work: 'Nothing to do with the project I know but I've got it off my chest now.' We argue it *is* to do with the project: the measures part of the curriculum is 'delivered' by teachers who have to take an overall view of courses and time management, for themselves and students. We have already noted that the teachers shared the students' perceptions of a constant rush. In one of the colleges, classes were timetabled back-to-back and in different parts of the site, so that the teacher had no alternative but to leave classes early or start them late. Teaching measures often involves particular equipment: ferrying weighing scales or measuring jugs around the site complicates the teacher's day. Topo and Mark, teaching in prisons, did not have to move from classroom to classroom – but Mark wandered the wings carrying materials and looking for students, and Topo, with full classes, had only 15 minutes' notice of who would be attending.

We believe these problems are not just accidents of the particular sites in which we worked: they are recognised by all the teachers with whom we have spoken, and it is possible that they are found in literacy and ESOL work as well as numeracy. Eamonn described how policy developments impacted on his working life: he joined the project because he had:

> a need to address, at a personal level, the dilemma brought about by the current trend to assess 'value for money' and 'quality' in teaching and learning in smaller and smaller units of time (the fact that you can show your students have made measurable progress at the end of their course from their initial assessment is no longer sufficient – you must evidence this progress weekly through the scheme of work, session by session in the lesson plan, which should reflect the Individual Learning Plans of all the participants, and virtually minute by minute if you are being observed ....) versus the merits of looser projects and tasks which allow students space to learn from and with each other. (Leddy, 2004)

So teachers and students are measured too. Employers are driven by the need to get the maximum 'output' (student achievements) from their staff, and in section 8 we discuss aspects of policy relevant to our project.

5.4 Where is the mathematics in measurement? Measures, technology and change

We have seen students splitting broadly into two groups: those who see little practical (everyday life) need for formal measurement skills and those who argue the skills are vital. The second group often have jobs or other contexts in which they developed the skills they needed. Measures, as usually taught in the classrooms in which we worked, are often therefore not seen as useful in themselves, but important rather for passing examinations and for helping children; it is no surprise then that students' self-assessment seems to be based on assessment by teachers and through tests. Measurement is potentially one of the most practical, applicable areas of the mathematics curriculum, yet the research team and many students agree that studying it remains dry and may feel pointless.

The skills of measurement, and what students perceive as their 'needs', are changing as technologies change. Government discourses revolve around what are perceived as the 'needs' of adults (and their workplaces), but those needs change as the cultures and technologies around us change. Supermarkets provide pre-packaged food; scales print out prices. Carpet shops send workers to measure up: those who work in the trade have strong skills in measurement, and those who don't rely on those who do. Competent cooks 'measure' ingredients by eye, taste and experience, rather than scales. We buy petrol and milk in litres, gallons or pints, but they are measured by machines. Geraldine, whom we quoted above arguing that classroom work on measurement is of immediate value in helping her save money, told us she weighs individually-priced goods such as lettuces in order to get the best value for her money. Geraldine defended her practice against critics among her family and friends who argued her time was worth more than the money she saved, but those critics may be right, we think. The weighing has been done; the shops themselves do not want significant variation in the weight/price ratio.

As noted above, Rudolf Sträßer has noted the disappearance of mathematics into modern technologies, with mathematics remaining invisible to the user under normal circumstances (Sträßer, 2003). His argument is not only about measures, but we found striking illustrations in the project. For example, Kamar distinguished between what is needed in Somalia and London. In Somalia, knowledge of litres is useful; in London: 'You don't need to use it. Everything is marked already.' Similarly, an ethnographic study of error-critical drug administration by experienced nurses found their calculation strategies to be tied to individual drugs in specific quantities and volumes, the way they are packaged, and the ways in which clinical work is organised; no actual measurement of drug quantities or concentrations is involved (Hoyles et al. 2001).

We had further support for Sträßer's analysis from Wood, an investment banker (Belmarsh). He explained why he wanted to improve his mathematics: 'I'm just pounds, percent' (that is, he is not familiar with other areas), but even within money and percentages he 'couldn't do anything' without a spreadsheet. Alison had difficulty believing him, and asked if he could find £38 as a percentage of £2,000: he answered, 'not without a spreadsheet'. Wood described the division of labour: if bankers wanted particular calculations for a customer, they asked spreadsheet specialists to set it up. The people appointing staff to roles such as Wood's 'won't touch maths graduates', because they 'want to teach you to do it [their] way'. The investment houses want people who sound and look confident and will learn quickly what is needed by the bank – and that is not, in that particular role, good mathematics; instead, 'You blag your way into the job'. Wood was attending the course in order to 'strengthen' his mathematics to be able to help his daughter in the future (she was five at the time of our discussion).

We address these issues again in the next section, on our proposals.

5.5 Summary

This section identifies some of the key issues raised in our research and explains our decision to focus on under-researched aspects of measurement which lie within the popular understanding of the meaning of measurement (length, capacity, weight/mass and time), thereby excluding money. We considered, first, students' perspectives on the use of measures (their existing skills and needs, and their views of the value and use of measurement). We found that while some saw measurement as fundamental to mathematics (a view shared by the research team], most were not interested in the practicalities of using measures; they saw it as important for passing examinations, and/or they wanted to help their children. Others stressed the importance of being informed and felt that 'to communicate with people, you do need measurement'. Students' perspectives on teaching and learning measures were remarkably consistent: good teachers were seen as caring about their students, fostering classroom cultures which support trust and open communication; the teacher-student personal relationship was seen as central (views also shared by the research team). They valued the mutual support they found in the classroom and bemoaned the lack of time available to study at their own pace. Most measured their own progress by their coverage of the curriculum and success in tests, rather than in terms of their increased ability to use measures outside the classroom. Teachers' perspectives on teaching and learning measures covered a range of areas: proxy measures; the use of decimal numbers in measurement; the measurement of time; the importance of discussion in class; misleading visual representations of objects and their measurement; the impoverished curriculum available to young 'low achievers'; and the chronic lack of time to teach at an appropriate pace in a target- and test-driven professional context. Time featured poignantly in another way too: students and teacher-researchers enjoyed working on measures of time, playing with it, indulging their curiosity.

Measurement skills and students' perceived needs are changing as technologies change with less need for direct measurement skills in some areas. The practicality and applicability of measurement does not, of itself, make it an interesting area to teach or learn for all students. All in all, measurement is revealed as a complex and somewhat contradictory area for teaching and learning: at once at the heart of mathematics and surprisingly absent, for some people, from activities which are commonly assumed to involve a lot of measurement, such as cooking, shopping and merchant banking.

6 New classroom approaches

In the second year of the project we concentrated on developing materials and a scheme of work to support both teaching and learning measures, and critical discussion of the meaning and social and historical development of measures. Materials are available on the website, copyright free, so here we focus on students' responses to some of the teaching and learning materials and activities, and our reasons for developing a new scheme of work, questions about measures to prompt discussion, and materials on the history of measures.

The approaches may not be new to some teachers; those who have started training and work under the funding arrangements of the 1990s (which shaped accountability, and therefore examinations and curricula) or since *Skills for Life* may find the ideas here less familiar. We argue that our project has gathered evidence for approaches which, however widely used, have not before been researched in adult numeracy education. The critical issue of how the work described here fits with policy and funding constraints is discussed in section 8.

6.1 Teaching and learning resources

To introduce the kinds of resources we have developed, we outline what happened when two were tried out by students. This will illustrate our sources for the more general comments we go on to make about the changes of classroom culture and apparent benefits of the sorts of work we have been developing. Some of the resources have been trialled by students only in their own classrooms, and others at the students' seminar on measurement; we draw on their comments as they used and critiqued the materials. We finish with a discussion of the possible limitations and difficulties of the sorts of work we are advocating. First, our two examples: a joint pottery and mathematics project and work on measuring using paces.

6.1.1 Measuring change: 'It's nothing to do with pottery, it's only got to do with maths'.
Topo Wresniwiro worked with the pottery teacher at Belmarsh to design a project based on the changing size and weight of tiles as they go through the stages of drying and firing over a period of several days. We imagine this joint work will not be possible in most sites, so the worksheet is not on the website, but the principle of measuring change may be accessible in other contexts. Abs and Whiteley made three tiles, cut to the same size and thickness, and inscribed a 10 cm line on each. The line was the focus for their work on changing length, and they also weighed the tiles at different stages. This is part of Abs' written account (we have standardised the spelling):

> Me and Whiteley went and joined [the pottery teacher] in pottery class to do an experiment is to make 3 tiles (brick). But I did not read the instruction properly. I went and got some clay and made 3 tiles; after I made 3 tiles, Whiteley then said that I have made a mistake – so I said to him explain to me what I have done wrong.

> Whiteley   "You're supposed to make a diagram, and before you make the tile you're supposed to estimate how much clay you're going to use"

> Abs: I told him ok I have made a mistake but I've already made 3 tiles and there's nothing I can do about it, but what we can do is get some more clay and

*estimate how much clay we're going to use to make 3 tiles. And then weigh
the clay we estimate, and measure the 3 tiles I've made. And then what we do
is to minus from the clay we estimated [to find the difference between the
estimated and actual weights].*

Abs proposed what many students do, when asked to estimate: measure first, then make a
retrospective estimate by rounding off the measurement. It is well nigh impossible to
estimate first, as many worksheets ask, if you have no familiarity with the measures; as
Kamar (Westminster Kingsway College) put it: 'The more you do, the more you have got the
experience, and the [...] more you use the measurement, you can estimate'. Abs and Whiteley
were interested enough in the project to engage in a debate and then continue it in writing –
an astonishing shift in the classroom cultures we are familiar with.

When Alison talked to them, the tiles were still losing weight and the lines were shortening.
The students told her the weight of one tile was 133.3 g: the scales were poor, so they had
weighed three tiles and divided that by 3 – that is, they had found an average, and a way to
deal with poor equipment which felt as though it would provide a more accurate measure.
Abs said: 'You wouldn't get points in grams'; he had developed a sense of the smallness of a
gram.

We asked whether their interest was in the pottery or the mathematics:

*It's nothing to do with pottery, it's only got to do with maths. All we've learned about
pottery is you lose weight. And every 10 centimetres, it loses one centimetre. If I was to
make something 100 centimetres, I'd have to make it 110 centimetres. (Abs)*

That immediate shift into talking about the content of the mathematics was typical; and in the
shift to making a general rule, Abs was extending the work from the immediate tasks to much
harder mathematics. When Alison looked doubtful about the 110 centimetres, the two
engaged in a debate; asked how it could be worked out; and when Alison said the only way
she knew would use algebra, they asked to see how she would do it. Abs then said he would
test his ideas with a new tile:

*Next week I'll do 11 point 1 [cm]. I didn't know I'm going to argue with [Whiteley] for
two weeks. He wanted a diagram and I didn't need to. The diagram didn't make no
difference. I wanted to do it quick.*

Whiteley said of one tile: 'So it's lost 25 grams, so it's 25 grams for 3 millimetres of length':
that is, he introduced ratio, not required by the worksheet.

This project seems from the outside to lack reference to 'real life': measuring the slow
changes in a tile is apparently pointless (though it is vital in the pottery industry). It is hard to
imagine most students 'arguing for two weeks' after a class about a mathematical problem.
Their interest was not in how to use measuring equipment (though the students found ways to
compensate for error) but in the processes of change. Measuring change is not included in
the curriculum at these students' level, and measures in the classroom are usually presented
as static facts. In contrast, mathematicians see measures as approximations, the level of
accuracy dependent on what is needed (you do get 'points in grams' in some contexts) and the
tools (whether equipment or mathematical strategies) available; and the need to measure
and predict change has always been a motivation in the development of mathematics, from

renaissance work on cannon ball trajectories to the futures market in the City.

'It's nothing to do with pottery': it is often tempting to see particular contexts as a sweetener for mathematics. For some students, no doubt the pottery, rather than the mathematics, would be the central point, and indeed most mathematics has been developed to deal with particular problems. But there are, for some, pleasures and curiosities in mathematics itself.

6.1.2 Measuring length in paces: 'It makes us developing.'

A class working with Eamonn Leddy set out to measure the length of their classroom using paces as a measure and making up their own methods. They experimented, then opted for using the length of three paces, divided by 3 (so like the group above, they found a reason to use an average). Here we quote from the students' discussion at the end of the lesson.

Rose   *How did you measure the average pace?*

Walanwal   *Mine is 90 metres feet, because I'm little bit taller than you.*

Tony   *More than a little bit!*

(Several voices laughing.)

Rose   *Wait, he is talking!*

Walanwal   *I take two steps, so it will be 90 [pause] 90 metres.*

Rose   *90 metres?*

Walanwal   *Uh huh, and I start from heel to bottom.*

Rose   *Where did you start, to measure the – to start the measurement of your feet?*

Walanwal made a mistake in naming units, but our point here is that the correct naming of units was an issue for the group: they needed to know the units to understand each other. Walanwal raises the critical issue of where a measure starts (this is comparable to setting zero on kitchen scales); some people start counting at the beginning of a ruler, ignoring the blank bit at the end, or see the length from, say, the 5 cm to 8 cm marks as 4 cm, because there are four marks on the ruler (cf. Nuñes & Moreno, 2000).

One group's paces included 15, 30 and 23.3 cm (70 divided by 3); the other's included 57 and 64 cm. The students debated the implausibility of the first group's results, and decided that probably they had discounted whole metres when they did the division calculation (for example, ignoring the whole metre in 1.9 m, and instead dividing 90 cm by 3, giving 30 cm).

The work took an hour and little seemed 'completed': no-one had enough time to measure the room. Eamonn was concerned that perhaps it had seemed chaotic, but the students disagreed:

Eamonn   *I deliberately set that up so that [...] you've got to decide how you're going to do it. [...] How did you find that?*

Rose   *It's good*

Tony   *Yeah, quite easy.*

Rose   *It's good, because it makes us to be able to think, and understand. It gives us knowledge.*

Hermione *It gives us knowledge.*

Mary   *Will it always be the same? No*

Carmen   *More knowledge.*

Tony   *I've got knowledge. [chuckles]*

Hermione *So we can help ourself, even when the kids are not there, we have to help ourself ...*

Rose   *... without any help or something. It makes us developing.*

Carmen said, 'Your mind just works harder, you're actually physically doing it and it's using the brain as well'. 'It makes us to be able to think, and understand', as Rose put it, is a benefit: these students valued the intellectual struggle of their work. Much of the more usual work for numeracy students in effect protects them from mathematics: questions are designed so that solutions are straightforward at the 'appropriate' level.

Again the task was not 'real' – to measure a room, it is easier to use a tape measure. But in both these examples, students became curious about methods, for both measuring and calculating; collaborated; used the language of mathematics and measurement; saw problems and solved them.

At the seminar on measurement students tried out most of our new proposals for classroom work, including the 'pace' work described above. Drawing on tape recordings, a video, photographs and the team's notes of the event, we go on to describe what seem to be the benefits of these new ways of working.

6.1.3 'You can explain yourself': working collaboratively on rich problems
More open-ended tasks draw on a wider range of the skills needed for measuring: approximating, estimating, establishing appropriate tools, deciding whether they are accurate enough and dealing with errors. Rather than each skill being set up as a new thing to learn (for example, a worksheet asking students to 'estimate then measure'), the skills are integrated.

The resources also support group work. By that we do not mean teacher-led 'whole class' work but students' own conversations in pursuit of methods and solutions, with space to make errors. We have heard Hotel and Foxtrot arguing for student-only time; Fergus (Belmarsh) extended the idea to shared projects:

What I would find beneficial is actually learning in a group ... So I think there can be a couple of times when the classroom is turned over the students, if it's more of a project base where we can actually see some product at the end of the lesson. But it doesn't put the individual student in the spotlight.

As students at the seminar worked on the problems, they shared difficulties and problem-solving strategies:

Look at this! [laughing] I'm confused here. How am I going to measure the arms? (Woman at the seminar)

I make that [calculating something] – Oh, I was right, I'd rubbed it out. (Woman at the seminar)

Being 'confused' is evidently not failure. This is a quite different discourse from that of more usual classrooms, where students' self-assessment relies on external assessment from the teacher or examination board. We saw above that Walanwal was put 'in the spotlight' ('90 metres feet'), but errors change their character when people are engaged in a shared endeavour. Here two students work on completing a bus timetable. The given information included journey times, the length of stops and a break at 12:30, and their discussion had some of the features of solving an algebraic equation (something + something + ... = 12:30):

Woman   *Mmm ... what we're doing, it's a bit more challenging.*

Man   *Actually it's getting a bit complicated isn't it?*

Woman   *Complicated. That's the first bus, yeah ... but that's 30 minutes ... One journey? going back.*

Man   *He'll [the bus driver] carry on, I should imagine ... 30 minutes, 9:45, 30 minutes journey, 10:15.*

Woman   *Getting confusing.*

Man   *Why's he only taking 15 minutes? ... Now you've arrived at Battersea, you've got to go to Vincent Square again, haven't you.*

Woman   *OK, so what do we do now?*

Man   *Wait a minute. We've done this wrong somewhere. If he gets ... Lunch hour. If you do a 15 minute journey, that'll take him to 12:30.*

(From seminar tape transcript).

In planning the students' seminar, Rose talked about the value of working without a book, implying that is what leads to learning:

Let's get people learning [...] doing this measurement, and you [students] can explain yourself. Where you are working, you know what the measurement is. When you are just working out you have it in your head. Better than looking at the book. That's what I want.

Rose's description of learning fits Vygotskyan theories (see appendix 4). 'Looking at the book' is, in contrast, part of what Sommerlad (2003) calls the 'learning patrimony': our inherited and still dominant pedagogies. 'You can explain yourself': where answers are neither fixed nor obvious, students talk to one another and hence use the language of measurement.

In Belmarsh and at the seminar several students tried out designing their own units of measurement. That requires students to name the units they invent:

> We put the strip [of card], that's one foot. We divided this one foot into other measurements. We have four fingers to make one foot. We use the small finger. [...] And one 1 lin, that's the length [of] one line [joint], of our finger, three of that make one finger. (Abdul, reporting back for a group at the seminar)

The foot, finger and lin were standardised: the group had made rulers with which they measured objects in the room. We asked whether this was really 'useful': standard measures already exist, so perhaps to create a new system is pointless. Abdul defended it:

> Yes, what makes it, because in case you have to measure and you have no ruler, you can make your own measurement, just note it down. When you go home, probably you can take a ruler, and just take your measurement, to compare that.

Measures are, indeed, arbitrary, but they can feel arbitrary in the sense of wilfully difficult to students who find it hard to engage with formal measures in the classroom. Here Abdul describes being inside his own arbitrary system. That is a flexible view of measures: they are useful, and both invention and conversion are possible.

So far we have said that open-ended projects, and others which, like the timetable, are closed but challenging, draw on a wide range of mathematics skills and support group work. Next we describe communication among students. We have seen that students value talking to each other about their work, but now we highlight other communicative modes. Sketches, gestures, notes, pointing to objects, moving things around, and direct comparisons of dimensions and weights were all more strongly in evidence in the more open-ended projects we developed; Abs' written dialogue is an example of introducing written argument (which has a long history in the writing of formal mathematics, but is rarely used in numeracy classrooms). As Gunther Kress (2000) puts it, different communicative modes have different affordances: what can be 'said with a picture, for example, is different from what can be said in spoken or written words. New ideas had to be explained to others, and findings recorded, without a worksheet controlling content or layout. We suggest that when ideas are communicated in ways chosen by students, they are more likely to be understood and incorporated into students' own ways of thinking.

We also found that mixed level work was the norm: the projects lent themselves to debate, to different levels of accuracy and to collaboration. Some are designed with extensions (for example, the timetable work); others have less precise suggestions for further work ('Would this work for much larger weights – for example, an aircraft carrier at sea?', in work on finding weight and volume by displacement, for example). One student found some of the available work at the seminar too easy: 'It was too simple for me, but a good place to start'. Another, who had GCSE mathematics, found the work on measuring with paces challenging. Overall, we argue that richer situations provide better opportunities for students to combine their skills and experience so that the notion of 'level' is less relevant.

Next we argue that students' work on these problems fits with wider views of the uses of mathematics itself, and therefore of mathematics education.

6.1.4 Developing mathematical awareness

For some, 'numeracy' is wider than mathematics. It means using mathematics critically, and being critical of mathematics itself: 'that is why we can say that numeracy is not less than maths but more. It is why we don't need to call it critical numeracy – being numerate is being critical' (Tout, 1997, p.13). That is not the dominant approach taken in England, where the curriculum defines numeracy as a list of specified and restricted elements of mathematics. We turn now to linking the kinds of work we have described above to perspectives on the teaching of mathematics in relation to its uses in society.

The materials described above are not drawn from 'real life', but the skills used reflect what is known of adults' mathematical problem-solving outside educational contexts, including collaborative work, using a mix of tools (both real tools and mathematical models), a mix of communicative modes and a mix of formal and informal methods appropriate to the contexts (Lave, 1988; Moll & Greenberg, 1992).

'Real life' is not a helpful construction if it is set up in opposition to the classroom (Tomlin, 2002b). Students' motivating aims include doing well in examinations (and therefore careers) and helping children with school numeracy: both depend, they believe, on success in the classroom. Real life is not separable from education structures, parenting or the demands of the employment market. We argue that the kinds of work described here may help students develop both a deeper understanding of what they must learn for examinations, and a more critical stance on the uses of mathematics in the wider society.

Lena Lindenskov analyses different discursive conceptions of the relationship of everyday life and mathematics education. In the context of a discussion of teacher education and the development of textbooks for adult numeracy education, she argues for a model in which:

> elementary mathematics – including number sense, skills in arithmetic and other basic mathematical processes – are to be found [...] in very many places and always in highly complex ways, close-knitted with situation, intention and perspective. [...] Mathematical elements might well be 'silent' and 'invisible'. Therefore which mathematics and how mathematics is contained [...] first has to become perceptible. It is not easy, and you have to have a certain type of attention – a certain mathematical awareness. [...] It is therefore a task for basic mathematics education to prepare the ground for this particular attention. (Lindenskov, 2003, p.150)

Owen, a Lambeth student, makes a very similar point as he describes dipping in and out of mathematical awareness:

> You're learning in the classroom, but [...] it's all around you. But if you don't look into it, it's there but it's not there. Like, take the length of this table, you get one, two, three, four, people there. But you are not going to take into consideration, you know, come in, one sit there, one sit there, one sit there [...] [Measurement] does not register as such, until you bring it up as a topic, and then you start looking at things. [...] And yes, occasionally it comes in handy, but then it's only when you use it you are going to sort of look at it that way. (Communications class discussion of measurement)

We argue that the work we have developed supports Lindenskov's 'mathematical awareness'. Without this perspective, mathematical assignments have:

> *a huge risk to discriminate [against] learners who do not come from highly educated families. [They] demand that the learners already have certain knowledge of and an interest in the everyday phenomenon that appears in the assignment.* (Lindenskov, 2003, p.150)

We turn now to a view from 1977. Hugh Burkhardt argues that in model building:

> *the most important single factor is that the student should want to know the answer – no sensible person toils without purpose. [...] The problem must be interesting and familiar with some clear pay off from the use of mathematics.* (Burkhardt, 1977, p.14)

We have described some students (Bob, for example) 'toiling without purpose' on measures, in the sense that their purpose may be gaining a qualification rather than directly applying new knowledge to practical tasks. Burkhardt describes problems in terms of five 'interest levels':

- Action problems concern decisions that will affect your own life.
- Believable problems: action problems for your future, or for somebody you care about.
- Curious problems need have no practical relevance, but intrigue you.
- Dubious problems are there to make you practise mathematics.
- Educational problems are special – though dubious, they illuminate some mathematical insight so well that no-one would throw them out.

Burkhardt argues that for many students applied mathematics has been almost entirely dubious. Both the pottery and timetable activities described above could be categorised as dubious, yet the students' engagement made the problems at least curious. When we listen to Abs and Whiteley arguing over the tiles, or to the two students writing a bus timetable ('Why's he only taking 15 minutes?'), the problems seem believable too, though neither affects students' lives. This surely has something to do with students' relationships not only to the problem itself but with each other. Burkhardt's comment is still relevant:

> *Our educational system has overwhelmingly emphasised individual work. In tackling realistic applications, progress seems to be much faster in groups at the formulation and interpretation stages, when ideas are needed.* (op.cit. 24)

The tidy, step-by-step model of the ANCC suggests that learned methods, rather than ideas, are needed. If the student progresses satisfactorily up the skills ladder, with the teacher providing 'appropriate' tasks at every step, the student will succeed. Most students do; our concern is that they are succeeding in something which has little relevance outside the world of the adult numeracy standards.

A discussion of word problems (teachers' usual means for bridging the mathematics classroom and the real world) in the context of a theory of situated learning leads Jean Lave to propose two new relationships:

> *The first involves rethinking the mathematization of experience – something that might also be termed the situating of math in ongoing activity – as a valuable end product of*

math education. This stands in contrast with the view that math must be 'everydayed'
as an initial condition for math learning. A second shift [...] is a move away from the
relation that looms so important because of its theoretical and institutional history –
that between the 'everyday', or 'concrete', and the 'theoretical', scholastic abstraction
of school math – towards a different distinction: that between things (real and
imaginary) that do and do not engage learners' intentions and attention, and give
meaning to the activity they are engaged in and definition to 'what's going on here, what
am I doing now?' The real trick may not be one of finding a correspondence between
everyday problems and school problems, but making word problems truly problematic
for children in school – that is, part of a practice for which the children are
practitioners. (Lave, 1992, p.87-88)

Lave argues too for teaching to link strong goals for learners with an 'improvisational'
approach for reaching them: in the course of exploring this approach new styles of
mathematics problems emerge (op.cit. 88). We have seen students' attention engaged as they
deal with 'truly problematic' problems, and we suggest that in contrast the ANCC proposes an
'everydayed' form of mathematics.

So we argue that in work on the team's resources we have seen students developing a
language for mathematics and mathematical awareness; finding problems curious and
believable (though not 'real life' in the sense of drawn directly from contexts outside the
classroom); working with others to formulate strategies and interpret findings; and becoming
practitioners in their own classrooms, with teachers who took Lave's 'improvisational'
approach.

Finally, we point to one particular feature of the approaches adopted by some of the students.
We take a notion of inverse problem-solving from Heinz Engl, who described the development
of new mathematics to analyse a wide range of particular problems, including modelling road
traffic, finding land mines, financial risk analysis and modelling a blast furnace (Engl, 2003).
The problems are ones where an effect is known, and the task is to look back for the cause
(or combination of causes). Solutions often require compromises. Mark Baxter proposed to
the team that we could write problems for basic skills students along these lines, to introduce
'thinking skills' as well as numeracy tasks. Independently, Liz Richards commented on a
class where it seemed that the students had learned how to find a volume but did not
recognise a situation in which that skill was required: 'How do we teach thinking skills in
maths?'

The materials we developed were not designed to require inverse problem-solving (though the
timetable discussed above does require working backwards). However, we found that
students created their own inverse problems in the ways they worked on the resources. The
two working on the timetable found their first suggestions were unsatisfactory and worked
back to find where to change their work; the students measuring their paces found their
answers were implausible and worked back to find their own error; Abs and Whiteley were
interested in using algebra when they realised their generalisation to other sizes of tile would
not work. In some classroom contexts these would be examples of mistakes; here, they were
just part of the work. New mathematics is (usually) developed in order to solve problems;
students developed strategies to deal with problems they encountered in their work.

We do not want to argue that closed, fixed-answer work on measures is always inappropriate.
People who want to find, record or communicate a length need to know the relationships

between the units and to convert between them. However, if that is all that measures mean in the classroom, we lose the profound connections between measures and the meanings of mathematics itself, and opportunities to develop problem-solving and thinking skills. As we have seen, students value the intellectual endeavour involved in becoming 'practitioners' (Lave, 1992) of measures.

6.1.5 Is that the answer then?

We can view the research team's own processes as inverse problem-solving. One of the critical issues was to establish the parameters of the research problem itself. Having established students' and our own critiques of our usual teaching and learning of measures, we went on to develop ways of thinking about measures and learning materials which seem internally consistent and which address the problems we found. Like the students, we were self-critical, talked a great deal about the problems and possible strategies, found we did not always understand each other fully or have a shared language for our concerns, brought different sorts of experience to the task and had varying levels of interest in different aspects of the problem.

However, as Heinz Engl (2003) pointed out, solutions often involve compromises. We do not feel that we have found 'the answer' to how to teach measures, in that it is not easy to work in the ways we have described.

First, we have not sufficiently explored the ways in which work which is less directly teacher-controlled may go awry. For example, one of the groups at the seminar who worked on measuring a room using their paces did not do the task we envisaged, but something rather different. We described above a group working with Eamonn, who designed the task, finding the length of individuals' paces with a view to then using their pace to measure the room length. At the seminar, a group working without a teacher more or less reversed that process: they measured the room with a tape measure, then paced it, and from that found the average length of a pace. This is Jeremy explaining what the group had done to a new person who joined the group:

> 9 metres 83 centimetres. You need the average of what everyone else has got. We worked [it] out. The average was all of the people who did it, their strides, you add them all together, then divide by the amount of people, people's strides.

This group did 'the wrong thing', but does that matter? In some respects the two groups did the same. They both used a tape measure to measure a length (of three paces, in the case of the first group; of the room, in the case of the second) then divided by the number of paces to find average pace length. But the first group found average pace length in order to use it as a tool in finding room length; for the second group, average pace length was itself the main target. Both used 'real' tools (tape measures, calculators) and mathematical tools (averages, division, addition) and collaborated to solve a problem to do with measures. Both groups, too, enjoyed themselves. In this case, then, the fact that the second group did something that did not match the task sheet does not matter, but there are times when it would. We suggest that the question of when such a difference matters should be discussed among students and teachers. It is crucial to the development of what Lindenskov (2003) calls mathematical awareness, and also to the more usual approaches to developing problem-solving skills in which we are told to return to the original question and make sure that our answers make sense. More open tasks are more likely to support discussion of what makes sense and whether the mathematical processes used fit the problem; right and wrong are to do with fitness for purpose rather than matching a bald number or measurement given in the *Answers* pages of a textbook.

So 'errors' in understanding the setting of the problem can be seen, like errors in calculations, just as a part of doing the work, rather than failures: they are triggers for changes to the mathematical model and for the development of mathematical thinking. When students are working out their own methods rather than simply doing what they are told (by the worksheet or teacher), things often take longer – and that leads to our second concern.

The more open-ended, problem-solving approaches we have described take time, and we have described students' and teachers' feeling that they already do not have enough of it. Because of the need to 'get through' the curriculum, Eamonn, the teacher with the group whose work on pace we described above, decided against completing all the stages of the work (see the website for extensions). There is no easy fit between the needs to: cover an examination syllabus, including practising the particular forms of questions found there; tick off completed curriculum elements itemised on lesson plans for the purposes of accountability to employers and funders; check that students are achieving the aims listed on their ILPs; and develop critical mathematical thinking. The ANCC is designed around a particular understanding of the meaning of numeracy; its itemised, isolated skills do not easily fit the integrated mathematical thinking we have described.

Next we outline more briefly the other resources available on the website: a scheme of work, a collection of measures problems, materials on the history of measures and data from the project.

6.2 A scheme of work based around measures

In our workshop at ALM 10 (Baxter et al. 2003), participants supported the idea, first raised by Liz Richards, of teaching number skills through measures, rather than teaching (almost abstract) number skills (whole number, then fractions and decimals) then putting them into contexts by introducing units of measure. Liz then designed for her own use a new scheme of work, which has since been adopted by some of her colleagues. It is available on the web, along with a worksheet by Eamonn on solving linear equations which illustrates the principle of using measures as the basis for the development of mathematical skills. Here Liz outlines the principles behind the scheme of work.

Reasons for development

The impetus to develop a new Scheme of Work was twofold. Firstly, I wanted a scheme of work that allowed me to introduce topics using measurement as the modeller. Secondly, I felt that my current scheme of work, which introduced number in the first term, measure, shape and space in the second term and handling data in the third term, did not help my students who had poor short term memory.

Principle: using measurement as modeller for number skills.

- Check 24+16 by drawing and then measuring 24 cm and then 16 cm on A3 paper.
- Model 3x8·5 by drawing and then measuring three 8·5 cm lines.

- Discover number bonds using balance scales.
- Find the factors of 24 by drawing several 24-cm lines and marking off equal amounts.

These are only a few examples. Once you get into the habit of thinking about how you might demonstrate a technique using measure the ideas come fast and furious.

Outline, discussion

My starting point was to have a rolling programme of topics. I settled on seven topic areas:

- Place value, ordering, estimating, rounding, reading numbers from scales.
- Understanding + and -, money and real-life problems, checking results, mental calculation strategies.
- Measures, shape and space.
- Properties of numbers.
- Fractions and decimals.
- Handling data.

The ANCC and associated staff development materials (e.g. DfES & Basic Skills Agency, 2001b) do not focus on overall course planning. The curriculum is presented in three areas, *Number, Measures, Shape and Space,* and *Handling Data,* and many teachers organise courses around those areas. We have seen that both students and teachers are frustrated by the lack of time available for consolidating new knowledge: the 'rush' of getting through the curriculum. By incorporating measures into work on numbers and handling data students will have more time for practising skills which, we have argued, are often not practised in life. (Terezinha Nuñes and Constanza Moreno (2000) make a similar argument for a closer link between measures and number, in their development of programmes of study in mathematics for deaf children.)

6.3 Word problems: supporting a critical discussion about how to develop and test knowledge of measures

Drawing on work by Jeffrey Goodwin for the QCA (2004), on how the format, wording and graphic design of a problem influence children's 'take' on it, we have written a collection of word problems to do with measures (available on the website). They are of varied styles, in several ways: closed and open; giving none, a little or all of the necessary information (so that some invite students to use their own information, or research it); needing perhaps two or three minutes' or two or three hours' work; illustrated or words only; drawn from examinations, textbooks and members of the team; and including work on the different measures (but not money) included in the curriculum. The idea is not that the problems are to be solved by students (though of course they may be used for that purpose), but that they offer a vehicle for a discussion of word problems. Our suggestion is that students sort the problems into three groups: *would try, wouldn't try,* and *don't know,* and discuss their categories both while sorting into groups and when comparing their groupings with others. We hope in this way to extend the kinds of discussions held among teachers and researchers (for example, Lindenskov (2003), Burkhardt (1977) and Lave (1992), discussed above) to students themselves. We do not imagine that students will agree with each other and thus provide a template for their teachers' work, but rather that a critical discussion of word problems on measures will help both students and teachers develop ways forward.

Students too write word problems, for themselves or their fellow students. When some students were still struggling with work which others had finished, Liz suggested that those with time should write problems. It proved to be popular with students, and in the following lesson all wrote problems. These can contribute to assessment; for example, one student wrote:

I have 6 tables. Each table is 26 cm in length. How long are the tables altogether?

The question reveals a misconception of the length of a centimetre, but also a thorough familiarity with the usual word problem genre (cf. Tomlin, 2002a)

6.4 History and measures

Developing materials on the history of common measures was entirely the research team's idea, rather than grounded in classroom or interview data. The materials centre on the history of metric measures and the measurement of time, but we attempt also to give some context for their development, alongside forays into much older history (for example, the Egyptian measurement of the circumference of the world, and the timing of the summer solstice at Stonehenge), and more recent difficulties (the loss of a spaceship caused by a mix of metric and imperial measures). The materials are on the website.

We have said that measures are arbitrary: for example, the metre is one ten-millionth of a quarter of the world's circumference, so that the French revolutionaries who commissioned the creation of the metric system claimed it was rational and based in the real, natural world – but base 10 itself is a human construction. We wanted to make available materials which present measures as human creations, developed in particular social, political and historical contexts. Liz had already included the history of metric measures on her own website (http://www.liz.richards.btinternet.co.uk); all the teachers sometimes referred to the origins of the metric system when explaining its structure. We found little published material suitable for our classrooms, and hope our materials will prove accessible and useful.

6.5 Continuing the discussion

We mention here too another group of texts included on the website: extracts from the project's data, including interview transcripts and classroom notes. They are there with two uses in mind. First, though only a small sample of our data, they may expand readers' feeling for the kinds of problems we address in this report and the evidence on which we rely. Secondly, they too can be used as reading material to raise discussion with students about their and their teachers' work on measures (and again, they can be edited to suit particular readers). We noted above that students may be reluctant to criticise their classes or teachers; perhaps presenting material from research will support critical discussion among those to whom the debate most matters.

6.6 Summary

The new classroom approaches presented and discussed in this section support collaborative work and developing mathematical awareness. We present a scheme of work using measurement as a modeller for number skills. We argue that students working on the team's resources have developed a language for mathematics and mathematical awareness, found problems curious and believable, worked with others to formulate strategies and interpret findings and become practitioners in their own classrooms, with teachers who took Lave's 'improvisational' approach. We also point out some of the limitations of our approach: it is time consuming and runs counter to the itemised, isolated skills that structure the ANCC; we have not sufficiently explored the ways in which work which is less directly teacher-controlled may go awry.

7 What have we learned about teacher research?

The project's aims included building research capacity through the use of teacher-researchers. In appendix 4 we review the literature on teacher research and discuss its relevance for the *Measures* project. Here we focus on team members' experience of the project. First, though, some practical issues which may be relevant to future practitioner research projects.

7.1 When shall we five meet again?

Five education providers contributed to making the project possible by releasing the teacher-researchers. Not surprisingly, they were not released for the same day each week (and in one case, the teacher-researcher was released for several part-days, equivalent to a whole day), and it was hard to find times to meet. This may perhaps be particularly difficult in numeracy, where there is a shortage of teaching staff and therefore it may be difficult for organisations to find cover at times that suit the research project. The team all worked in London; had we been more scattered, it would have been even more difficult to meet as often as we needed.

7.2 Hunting measures at entry levels

The teacher-researchers in FE worked with several different numeracy and mathematics courses, up to A-level GCE mathematics, and those in prison worked with mixed-level numeracy groups. There were times, then, when a particular teacher-researcher was not working with students on measures at entry levels. It is likely that some skills, such as addition, or some contexts, such as money, are much more integrated through every lesson.

The focus on measurement at particular levels therefore restricted our database, though aspects of that restriction became research issues: why is there a mathematics graduate in an entry level 3 numeracy class? Why do measures seem so separated from, say, data handling? How does the teacher's entry level 3 scheme of work mesh with the individual learning plan of someone who is not much interested in measure? How come many people with level 3 and 4 qualifications cannot estimate metric measures?

7.3 Teacher-researchers or teacher-fieldworkers?

The NRDC has a distinction between practitioner-researchers and practitioner-fieldworkers (Barton and Papen, 2005). Within the *Measures* team we used the term teacher-researchers, although only one took a Masters research methods module, one of the distinctions between 'researcher' and 'fieldworker' in the early NRDC conception of the roles. Our research brief was explored, narrowed in some respects and widened in others in team meetings. All the team members – teacher-researchers, researcher and director – had years of experience teaching adult numeracy; the teacher-researchers were highly qualified in mathematics, and had experience of teaching mathematics to higher levels. In a project directed towards a particular aspect of mathematics, that was extremely valuable. The project was unusual in having a team of teacher-researchers working together on the same research questions, rather than each having an individually designed research project. Working in a restricted field in which we found little prior research (in any methodological tradition), all the team contributed to the establishment of key concepts, questions and research tools.

Next the teacher-researchers describe aspects of their experience of the project. First Liz Richards describes the practical business of data collection and course development, then Eamonn Leddy describes some of the shifts in thinking generated through team meetings. Topo Wresniwiro records the shift to seeing himself as a researcher, and finally Mark Baxter gives an overview, looking from the project itself to its meanings in terms of policy and practice.

7.4 Liz Richards: data collection and the development of new work

I wanted to take part in the measurement project for three reasons. First, I had been teaching for a few years and felt it was about time that I did something a little bit different. Secondly, I was aware that I was least satisfied with the way I taught the measurement part of the syllabus; the project would give me time for reflection which the increase in [teaching] contact time and paperwork no longer allowed; and thirdly, I had worked with some of the team members before and therefore was confident that the project would be worthwhile.

In the first year most of the time was taken up with writing copious notes of each session I did with students that involved measure. I started by trying to take notes during the lesson but soon realised that this was not possible unless I ignored the students so I had to just write down keywords and hope that I would remember what the keyword meant. It was crucial to write the notes immediately after the class – otherwise the more subtle aspects of students' comments and work were forgotten, but some of my teaching sessions were back to back, and so it was often two hours before I could write the notes, which made what I could recall a lot less accurate. We all generated a lot of data and after about four months it was decided that we would just concentrate on making detailed notes on certain aspects of students' learning. I found it almost impossible just to concentrate on and then remember one particular aspect of a student's learning without ignoring what else was going on in the classroom. I tried to record sessions, which my students were happy for me to do, but I could not position the microphone to pick up all the interchanges and usually just heard my twitterings.

In the second year we concentrated on interviewing students, thinking about materials that might aid the learning of measure and organising student discussions. This gave me the time to develop a scheme of work, which I hope will integrate students' understanding of measurement into the syllabus and make me feel more satisfied with this aspect of my teaching.

7.5 Eamonn Leddy: shifts in the project's focus

Initially our concept of 'measurement' was very inclusive and we discussed a lot of issues around teaching adults, in general, their common difficulties, 'why measurement?', 'isn't ALL maths measurement?' cultural variations, assessment and accreditation, the decimal system etc.

Later, for a while, we narrowed this down to looking at measurement, for our purposes, as only being that which involved measuring instruments or their replacement by informed estimation. This is when we started to develop some of our own more open-ended tasks, leading to more classroom discussion, communication and cooperation. Out of the classroom this led to discussions about time and evaluation constraints imposed by target-led and achievement-funded regimes. It 's all about getting the right balance... – as I get older I realise that this is the meaning of life, the universe and everything!

We established some themes and further research issues:

- There is a problem with lack of opportunity for students sufficiently to practise measurement and estimation (hence the new scheme of work).
- Students with vocational experience come with much more prior knowledge and 'common sense' approaches both to problem solving and appropriate methods and degrees of accuracy required. (How do they acquire that?)
- Mathematical problem solving needs not just mathematical skills, but also social and other prior skills! (How do we address that?)

7.6 Topo Wresniwiro: perspectives at the start and end of his work with the project

7.6.1 At the start
I joined NRDC about three weeks ago. Both my education manager and my students have been supportive and cooperative: without them this project will be difficult to do. I have made a start by giving them a questionnaire, trying to find out from them the 'what' and the 'why' we are doing measurement. In the next few weeks, I'm going to incorporate numeracy in pottery class and later in cookery. In the next meeting, I hope, I'll be able to report how we are getting on with our project ...

7.6.2 At the end
I am still learning every day; learning from the good practices of other teachers and the students' inputs, as well as from other researchers, is beneficial for my own professional development. I have become more alert and aware of how the students think, express or find ways of solving problems as they encounter them. Also I examine more now how they learn and absorb the explanations or information they receive: do they just absorb what they are being told without raising any questions? Or, are they curious and are going to pose a question, 'Why' or 'How'? To discover how other people learn greatly interests me. It is because we are all different, brought up in different environments, accustomed to different surroundings and opportunities that make us what we are. With our own individual experiences and knowledge, each of us has different ways of tackling problems. There is an awful lot to be learnt and discovered out there.

I tremendously enjoyed attending my first conference, the 10th ALM international conference in Strobl, Austria. As our team presented our research, I was nervous. The programme was packed, and I met interesting people, researchers and teachers alike. During the course of the conference I exchanged ideas and discussed several topics of interests and learned from their experience. Each time I attend research seminars, conferences or meetings, I discover that I have something new to think about. Research as a whole certainly feeds my intellectual curiosities. As a newcomer to this field of research, I definitely see a gap between teacher-researchers and researchers.

I enjoyed taking a research methods module at the Institute of Education, University of London, and went on to take other modules too. Now I want to continue with research, perhaps through a practitioner-led research project.

7.7 Mark Baxter: bewilderment, enrichment and the government's aims

I had been teaching numeracy in a local prison for five months when I first heard about being a teacher-researcher. Researchers were looking for teachers to report back on their classes and they were especially interested in the teaching of measurement. I had taught fine art for many years but, feeling that I should be doing something more useful, I had made a move into teaching basic skills. I was new to the field and keen to do anything to gain more experience. But this also felt right. I enjoyed teaching measurement to the prisoners. I was always eager for them to get beyond the basics and onto measurement. I then felt that I was teaching them something useful, or was it more personal? I hated maths vehemently at school unless I could see its practical purpose. As a teacher of numeracy to adults I now thought measurement was a highly relevant topic in everyday terms and surely everyone else did. (Subsequently many students' attitudes have challenged this.) So following an intriguing telephone conversation and an exhilarating interview I became a teacher-researcher ...

(Difficulties in numeracy work at the prison, described above, led Mark to leave.)

And what of being a teacher-researcher? It had been a very rewarding experience. Having to edit my teaching notes for someone else to read made me much more reflective. There was a slight relief at not being the only one who had to make sense of all the conflicting notes ... The other members of the research team were experienced basic skills teachers who were inspirational for a beginner like me. Every meeting was a chance to talk about education in broad terms. Away from the workplace there was less tendency to talk about details. Ideas were exchanged and there was fresh input from those teaching in different environments. On the downside, the chaos of the prison situation meant that I had little to report back ...

With the pressure from all quarters up high to make people pass examinations not only was the relevance of measurement within the context of the core curriculum to people's everyday lives questioned but so inevitably was the core curriculum. Was the research to back up the government's aims with some fine-tuning? But what if it had major criticisms? Would they be noticed or ignored? But perhaps in a way that sums up what being a teacher-researcher meant to me. A bewildering but enriching experience that provoked more questions than it provided answers.

In slightly amended form, Mark's reflection on the experience of being a teacher-researcher was later published: Baxter (2003).

7.8 Summary

In this section we have discussed issues around the key role of teacher-researcher in our project and the teacher-researchers have reflected on their experience on the project.

8 Policies

Here we comment on the effects of policy and management structures on the classrooms in which we worked. Our project had its life in particular conditions which impact on the recruitment of students, the curriculum offered to them and teachers' scope for changing practice – that is, in different managerial or policy conditions, our findings might have been quite different. Our account here is not theorised, in that we have not referenced research in the field of educational policy, though that would clearly be relevant. Rather, we pull together those particular features of policy and management which have been noted in the report as having some impact on teaching, learning and research.

We start with the impact on students and teachers of targets for achievement in numeracy, and then discuss questions of motivation for learning, models of classroom teaching and finally the view of numeracy given in the curriculum.

8.1 Meeting targets

Three sorts of targets, and possible mismatches between them, concern us here: students', teachers' and the government's. The targets are intended to contribute to the measurement of progress, but rather than measuring distance travelled, they set fixed points to be reached.

One means of measuring progress was the achievement of targets in students' ILPs. We did not ask students to discuss their ILPs with us, but we must note that at least sometimes students were gamely working on topics in which they were not much interested. If your reason for taking up adult education had nothing to do with numeracy, as was the case for some of the participants, and if you have no need for formal skills in measure other than that generated by the test at the end of the course, then the meaning of an 'individual' learning plan, with its connotations of personal choice, must be in doubt.

The government's own achievement of its targets is also measured, through students' achievements in the national tests:

> As an education or training provider, you will understand better than anyone the difficulties of engaging adults in literacy, numeracy or language learning. Our research shows a marked reluctance on the part of most non-learners with weak basic skills to go into any form of learning. There are emotional barriers such as lack of confidence, fear of failure and not wanting to return to 'school', as well as practical concerns such as travel, cost and childcare to overcome. We are looking to raise the basic skills levels of 750,000 adults by 2004, and 1.5 million adults by 2007. It's a big challenge. The launch of the Get On campaign has seen over 150,000 new learners passing a test in literacy or numeracy since the campaign started last August. (ABSSU, 2003)

Institutions have been asked both to expand provision (that is, not only provide courses, but persuade more people to study numeracy: poorly attended courses are closed) and to encourage students to enter for tests. We look first at the question of need, which has driven expansion.

Survey evidence suggests that numeracy difficulties are widespread, though the design of some surveys may be suspect (cf. Coben, 2001). The *Skills for Life* survey found that adults' own assessment of their numeracy did not match the test results. 67 per cent of those with entry 1 or lower level numeracy (that is, assessed as weaker in numeracy than many of the students whose work is discussed here) felt that they were very or fairly good at number work. The survey writers propose that many people do not realise the negative effect this has on their lives; have found jobs that demand only the appropriate level of skill; or 'have developed coping strategies so their limitations are not exposed' (DfES, 2003). Those limitations are exposed through testing. The survey used the ANCC levels as descriptors for respondents' capabilities. However, John Gillespie (2004), one of the designers of the survey, comments that being 'at a given level' is not meaningful for many individuals, 'as levels embody predetermined assumptions about progression and relative difficulty'.

The adult population of England seems not to agree with the government's view that it has a problem with numeracy. Government discourses revolve around what are perceived as the needs of adults, but those needs change as the cultures and technologies around us change. We argue that the adult population of England may not be deluded in thinking that their measurement skills are adequate to their needs, if those needs are cast in terms of 'everyday' (outside education) life: it is when their numeracy is tested, or they want to help their children with school work, that their skills are inadequate. Research evidence suggests that 'basic' numeracy skills (as defined in the core curriculum) are less necessary for adults in 'everyday' life than ever before. As mathematics becomes invisible, embedded in technologies (Sträßer, 2003), so the need for the numeracy skills of the sort in the lower levels of the ANCC is reduced.

We must not overstate this argument: people will always want, for instance, to know they are not being cheated, or to be able to help their children with their own tests. But there are other very important contexts where numeracy skills may be critical – decisions on mortgages, voting in the EU referendum, trade union policy and managing businesses, for example. Measures remain important in many work environments, though they frequently depend on the use of measures and equipment which are specialised to that particular function and therefore are not taught in generic numeracy courses (van Groenestijn, 2003, p.12-13).

The ANCC seems to be founded on two pillars: the National Numeracy Strategy for primary schools, which has steered both content and pedagogy, and a view of the mathematics which adults are taken to 'need'. The national curriculum (in schools) was itself influenced by the Cockcroft report (Cockcroft, 1982, p.85) which referred to adults' uses of mathematics as a source for a view of the requirements of the schools curriculum. In the processes of translation from mathematics in the social worlds of adults to primary schools and back to adult education and training, the curriculum has lost some of its justification in terms of adults' needs.

Mieke van Groenestijn suggests that the meaning of numeracy has been narrowed:

> *Since many adults in adult education have no good memories of school mathematics, 'numeracy' courses were started, in particular in the USA, Australia and Great Britain, to indicate 'practical mathematics'. The emphasis in numeracy courses was mainly on how to use basic mathematics in real-life situations and to feel comfortable with numbers. This, in fact, reduced the broad meaning of the concept of numeracy to doing simple operations and computations with numbers and measurement.* (van Groenestijn, 2003, p.11)

She argues for a numeracy curriculum based on 'managing situations':

> *In adult numeracy education the focus should not only be on learning mathematics, but also on learning how to manage mathematical situations and on acquiring new knowledge and skills in out-of-school situations.* (op. cit.:17)

In contrast, the ANCC's focus is on in-school situations: curriculum elements are largely derived from the schools' mathematics curriculum and the National Numeracy Strategy rather than from out-of-school situations. It does claim, however, to draw on students' contexts; we return to this question later. First, we illustrate the effort to persuade us that we need the numeracy of the ANCC:

> *People actually don't think they have a problem [...] They may have built up skills in particular hobbies or activities, such as darts, but really they struggle with more everyday, mundane activities. These could be work-related problems, such as a carpet fitter ordering the wrong length of carpet, or more domesticated issues such as working out the correct measurements of a baby's milk formula, or getting a child's medicine dosage right.* (Susan Pember, quoted by Allen, 2004)

These are possible problems, but we have counter-examples. The carpet fitter in our study had measurement skills well beyond his supposed numeracy level. The only person in our research to mention measuring medicine was Kamar, a mathematics graduate; research shows that for nurses, little measurement is involved in preparing drug dosages (Hoyles et al. 2001). We suggest that both Ms Pember and Kamar were using their own mathematical knowledge to persuade us of the need for measurement skills at fairly low levels of the curriculum, rather than identifying actual problems in society. As we have seen, it is difficult for those skilled in the use of common measures to imagine life without them. 'Managing mathematical situations' suggests a more complex view of adults' needs. It is not that measures are unimportant: as we have argued above, very nearly everything in our lives is measured. We need perhaps again to rethink the meaning of 'basic' (as in 'basic mathematics', or 'adult basic skills'). In the ANCC mathematics is conceived as a straightforward hierarchy, the bottom levels being basic. Taking a critical and dynamic view of measures, rather than seeing them only as facts and skills to be acquired, and deriving contexts and skills from the mathematics in students' lives or the use of measures in the wider society would generate a different list of needs.

We turn now from 'need' to the expansion of provision. The lower level of demand for numeracy has meant that it has often been provided as mixed-level courses. Provision has expanded quickly as organisations strive to meet the targets and use the *Skills for Life* developments as a means to expand their organisations generally. The expansion means that classes may be more differentiated in level, so it is possible (or perhaps expansion leads to the illusion that it is possible) to teach groups at one level, or perhaps across two levels: and so a whole class may be working through the entry level 3 curriculum. (Again, we write here from London, with a large population and a long history of provision; we recognise that other areas have different histories and patterns of provision.)

But there is a contradictory trend. We have noted that in what seems to be an effort to recruit more students to numeracy, though it may also be for other funding reasons, some colleges have organised numeracy into a Return to Study (or similar) package with, for example, literacy and IT. While this may have the advantage of making space in which students can get to know one another and develop mutual support (we have not explored this), it undermines the 'levelling' of groups in terms of numeracy. Since students are primarily assessed on their literacy skills, the IT and numeracy skills ranges may be comparatively wide. Further, some students have little real interest or personally identified purpose in studying numeracy (though none in the project has been resentful: a tribute to students' resilience and openness, to the skills of their teachers, or to both).

On the other hand, where potential students are available for only a short period, there are different organisational problems. Prisons have a high turnover and prisoners are frequently moved, even if they are serving long sentences:

> *[To] ensure that the transfer of prisoners around the prison estate does not prevent them from making progress in their learning [...] establishments are advised to place any necessary 'holds' on prisoners who are engaged in education programmes. All prisons are required to provide a core curriculum of subjects like basic skills, IT and social and life skills, a prisoner who is transferred midway though one of these subjects is likely to be able to continue at the receiving prison. Basic skills are assessed using a national test which is now available weekly in most prisons. We are therefore making provision consistent and allows for continuity of learning. [sic]*
> (Offenders' Learning and Skills Unit (DfES), 2003, formerly known as Prisoners' Learning and Skills Unit).

The PLSU here asserts that the combination of 'holds', a core curriculum and making tests available weekly will generate continuity of learning. Aside from the elision of any potential disjuncture between teaching and learning, this raises key questions. The ANCC sees students as 'bringing' their context to the numeracy course: what happens to the student's 'context' that s/he 'brings' to the prison? The work involved for teachers in coming to know relevant contexts for students is considerable, and it is unlikely that, with a fast turnover of students, teachers can keep up. What happens to the culture of the classroom when the national test is 'available weekly' – and particularly, what happens to teachers' expectations of students and to students' aspirations? There are bound to be difficulties when prisoners are frequently moved, and problems of prison overcrowding and staff (prison officer) deployment are beyond the scope of our project. But we raise here the temptations of a discursive match between a bullet-pointed curriculum and the short-stay (or unpredictable stay) world of prison. A prisoner who either has been assessed, or can be assessed quickly using the new assessment tools, who is likely to be with the tutor for only a short time, and for whom the tutor needs to show progress in order to meet targets, can be 'mapped' with the bullet points of the curriculum. The PLSU seems here to describe a production line, along which prisoners are passed, learning bullet points as they go, with an uninterrupted stream of newly accredited students appearing at the end of the line. This was not the practice of the two prison education departments in the project; nevertheless we recall Ade, entered for tests he found easy without having had any teaching.

Achieving the targets relies on organisations' recruiting students and on students' studying the required curriculum and passing the associated tests. Between the two are the teachers, trying to meet individuals' interests as well as examination requirements, ferrying equipment from building to building in, apparently, no time, endlessly planning and recording their own and students' work against checklists and plans. All the teacher-researchers sought time to think about their work, in collaboration with others with like interests. That should, surely, be possible, particularly in London where travel is comparatively easy and there are perhaps more numeracy teachers than anywhere in the country. What made it possible was paid release for the project; within their usual working lives, there is no time for professional development other than that geared to 'delivering' the curriculum. For teachers to develop new understandings of a curriculum, and work on delivery models with colleagues who teach the same students, demands time and space for thinking and experimenting.

8.2 From 'students' motivation' to 'motivating learners'

Here we discuss the shift from 'students' motivation' to 'motivating learners' as those terms appear in management and policy discourses, rather than their meanings in, for example, psychology. This is not a discussion of how people learn, but a discussion of how learning and studying are talked about.

We have quoted several students who did not themselves seek out a numeracy course, but were funnelled into numeracy by college or prison course structures. We have seen too that financial means are used to encourage demand, with payments to prison students for taking examinations, and to younger students for attendance at college. Both systems use financial 'motivation' in part at least to enable the government to meet its targets.

Both 'motivation' and 'learning' are terms with shifting meanings. In the 1970s and '80s, students' 'motivation' meant the collection of circumstances that had led to their enrolling for courses; 'good practice' (in government discourses as well as practitioners'), was to 'negotiate the curriculum' around what students wanted to learn (many would challenge what 'negotiation' meant in practice, but the rhetoric was there). Now 'motivation' seems to mean something more like 'encouragement' – that is, students lack their own motivation and we (government, teachers, referral agencies) have to provide it.

Government discourses adopt the term 'learners' rather than the 'students' we use in this report. But to 'learn' something implies success (when you have learned, you understand or remember, or can use or do, something); and learning need not be done deliberately. In contrast, 'study' and 'student' imply conscious decision and endeavour. It is possible to study unsuccessfully without the failure being your own fault – you may have a poor teacher, for example. 'Learners' seem not to have the possibility of failure. The term separates 'learners' of literacy, numeracy and ESOL from university or FE 'students'. That is, it distinguishes 'basic' level students from higher level academic and from vocational and leisure courses, invoking the discourses of social class and intelligence. Some argue in favour of the label 'learners' as the less teacher-centred word: so, for example, a 'learner' might be someone studying entirely independently. But the developments around *Skills for Life* are not about independent study, but rather 'motivating' people to take up courses in order to achieve targets set by the government.

8.3 One size fits all?

The curriculum up to level 1 is founded on the National Numeracy Strategy for schools at key stages 1–3. It is reasonable to look to schools research for pointers to consider in researching pedagogy in adult numeracy education. As a large scale reform, the National Numeracy Strategy appears to have been effective in promoting pedagogic change, but much of this change has been at surface level and it is difficult to draw clear conclusions about the impact of such change on student learning (Earle et al. 2003). Research shows that whether teachers use a range of teaching approaches that take into account the nature of what is to be learnt, for example concepts as opposed to procedures, and consider the needs of learners at different stages of their school careers, does impact on learning outcomes (Linchevski & Kutscher, 1998). This suggests that a 'one size fits all' view of pedagogy should be avoided, and indeed recently a more flexible approach has been advocated for the implementation of the National Numeracy Strategy.

It may be claimed that we do not have a 'one size fits all' policy in adult education: students 'bring their contexts', and teachers should adapt their teaching accordingly. However, particular forms of lesson plan and pedagogy have been promoted. We have found that one size does not fit all: though most students are content with their courses (whether or not they *wanted* to study numeracy) some are not. The 16–18 groups had the same teachers, working to the same curriculum, as the older students in our study, and their teachers knew the size they offered did not fit the younger students. That does not rule out the possibility that there is, somewhere, a perfect way to teach, which would ensure everybody learned: but the enormous diversity of adults' contexts, prior knowledge and preferred ways of learning makes it unlikely.

Of course we ourselves are advocating approaches to the teaching of measures. We hope though that rather than a recipe for success, our proposals will be read by teachers as possibilities, with their own contexts and particular students in mind.

8.4 'Bringing together the skills framework and the learner's context': difficulties with the curriculum

> *Each individual learner will come with their own set of priorities and requirements, and these must be the starting point of their learning programme development. [...]*
>
> *This adult numeracy core curriculum provides the skills framework, the learner provides the context, and the teacher needs to bring them together in a learning programme using relevant materials at the appropriate level, to support learners in achieving their goals.* (DfES & Basic Skills Agency, 2001a, p.9)

Here we review the ANCC's presentation of the relationships between the skills framework, students and teachers. First, a reminder: our project worked only in 'stand alone' courses; our comments here are limited to courses which are not linked to a specific context (car maintenance, vocational training, family numeracy or tenants' rights, for example).

We discuss in turn the statements that 'the learner provides the context' and that the curriculum provides the content.

Students' individually identified needs (in relation to measurement) are often to pass a test, or help children, and 'getting through' a standard curriculum is itself then a response to the student's 'context'.

One response to the desire to address individuals' specific interests is to organise the course largely around individual teaching. The evidence from the two prisons is that although the materials were individually geared to students' needs, that is not the same as working within students' contexts. It can be a particularly sharp issue: for example, Mark Baxter discussed tensions between teachers' possible approaches: trying to offer students a new and creative way into mathematics, or using their existing knowledge, including (for some) experience in weighing and pricing drugs. But even without the special tensions of prison education, it is difficult to organise numeracy around individual interests. To do so may require the student, teacher or both to develop new teaching and learning materials; more often, the student is offered materials that seem to the teacher to address some of the skills required. Context often determines the mathematics to be used; outside-classroom problems are not always transferable to classroom contexts.

It is in the nature of a test-driven curriculum that measures, for example, are studied by all students, even though few request them. The curriculum's advice is that the student's priorities are to be the 'starting point' of their learning programme; that suggests a recognition that in organising whole-class work, personal priorities may be compromised as the course develops.

We suggest thinking about context differently. In work on the more open-ended activities that we have described, students engaged with the work in ways that mirror our engagement with real (outside the classroom) problems: creating their own questions within the activity, going at their own speed, developing the language needed to debate problems with each other, collaborating and finding their own ways of understanding tasks. 'The learner' of the ANCC is an abstraction, a singular representation of all students; we propose instead 'the students provide the context', or, better, 'the students create the context'. It is still important that students be able to seek assistance with particular personal needs, but that need not detract from working towards classrooms in which students can be known more individually because they are in working relationships with others.

We turn now to the notion of a unitary skills framework – the content of the ANCC. There is a growing body of research, both theoretical and empirical, arguing that the development and use of mathematics are dependent on context (see, for example, Ernest, 1998; Lave, 1988; Skovsmose, 1994). The lists of skills of which the ANCC consists therefore do not (fully) 'provide the content', because they are divorced from context. The contexts that seem in this study to influence students' work are of three interdependent sorts:

1   The mathematical context (for example, fixed or open answers, or standard or investigative methods).
2   The task context (cf. Burkhardt (1977) and Lindenskov (2003), discussed above).
3   Group work which generates a shared context for mathematical problems and their solution, and supports students' relationships with each other.

It is beyond the scope of this study to propose particular changes to the underlying philosophy of the ANCC. We do, however, hope that this report provides some evidence of the complexities of teachers' and students' dealings with measures – a tiny sample of the social construction and use of mathematics. The 'basic' skills of measurement are not only those in the curriculum, but include those of dealing critically with measures as they are used in society.

8.5 Critical analysis, economic development, democracy and aesthetics

Ten years ago Martin Yarnit argued that with the loss of a 'vanished era' of adult education, collective learning had been diluted into 'student-centred' learning:

> But student-centred learning has a fatal weakness at its core. It demotes the collective in favour of a largely vapid notion of the education consumer [...]
>
> The problem [...] is that the last 15 years have seen the devaluation of education for personal and social development and the rise of a narrow form of vocational education, underpinned by a bureaucracy of learning outcome measurement. (Yarnit, 1995:72–3 and 75)

Yarnit advocated a lifelong learning system which would support the development of critical analysis and of the capacity and ideas for individual and collective social and economic development, including skills for work. The view in recent policy of numeracy as a fixed and ordered list of skills and facts, divorced from its uses and users, both undermines the development of flexible, powerful mathematics and misrepresents its uses in society; its narrowness and rigidity leave students, we have argued, identifying their progress only through teachers' comments and examination results, rather than through changes in their own use of mathematics and further developing their own intellectual, critical power.

Next we highlight two recent developments, in Scotland and Sweden, which are of value in suggesting alternative conceptions of an adult numeracy curriculum. Adult literacy and numeracy policy for Scotland is currently being developed, and explicitly recognises the importance of context for the meanings of literacy and numeracy:

> What constitutes an adequate standard of literacy and numeracy has not remained static throughout history. Literacy and numeracy are skills whose sufficiency may only be judged within a specific social, cultural, economic or political context. Our own definition, which received strong support in the consultation process, tries to take account of this:
>
> 'The ability to read and write and use numeracy, to handle information, to express ideas and opinions, to make decisions and solve problems, as family members, workers, citizens and lifelong learners.' (Scottish Executive, 2003)

In defining literacy and numeracy as 'complex capabilities rather than a simple set of basic skills' (Learning Connections Adult Literacies Team, 2003), the Scottish approach addresses some of our concerns about the formulation of the adult numeracy core curriculum in England (see also Coben, 2005).

Our second example draws on recent research and policy development work on adult-numeracy, carried out for the Swedish government by Lars Gustafsson and Lars Mouwitz (2004), to highlight issues which lie beyond the scope of our own research but resonate with Yarnit's wider purposes for adult education. The authors of this wide-ranging study come to findings strikingly similar to our own. They point to the often-extensive learning adults have gained in outside-education environments, and suggest that:

> school mathematics [that is, formal education in mathematics, including as an adult]

may sometimes interfere with the adult's informal knowledge, and the adult will then produce lower test results after completing the course than before. (op. cit:4)

Further, 'research has often drawn attention to the gap between "school mathematics" and the mathematics that adults actually use or need in a range of life situations' (op. cit:5). Gustafsson and Mouwitz discuss too the embedding of mathematical models in artefacts, rendering the mathematics invisible; and they challenge the presentation of lifelong learning as an individual life project rather a collective project.

But we want to use Gustafsson and Mouwitz to introduce two particular themes which were not so directly addressed in our research. First, they contrast the experience of school mathematics as a 'life-inhibiting stigma' (op. cit:6) with mathematics as:

a domain for a particular kind of aesthetic experience, it provides moments of clarity and beautiful patterns that can create highly euphoric feelings of insight and overall understanding. (op. cit.:6)

Not much to do with measures, perhaps – but we recall that measures are at the heart of mathematics. We can easily believe that 'real' mathematicians experience euphoria in their work, yet why do we so easily assume that adult numeracy students are not, and will not become, real mathematicians?

Secondly, we have argued that as society changes, measures change too: adult numeracy courses should help adults to keep up with change and maintain a critical stance. Gustafsson and Mouwitz challenge such presentations of 'the society of tomorrow as if it existed today': it is 'in conflict with the democratic idea that man creates his future through his own activities' (op. cit.:3). It is an effort for teachers and researchers to 'keep up' ourselves with the demands of present policy; we value wider perspectives such as this, reminding us to think more widely and freely about our work.

8.6 Summary

In this section we have shifted our focus beyond the immediate concerns of the project in order to explore the policies which shaped it. We conclude that the view of numeracy as a set of de-contextualised skills and facts is damaging to students and teachers, and to society in general.

9 Implications for practice, policy and research

There has been very little research into the teaching and learning of measures, in school or post-compulsory education. So much work remains to be done that we cannot itemise particular contexts, topics or theoretical questions which need further study – the list would be too long. Here we restrict ourselves to six broad suggestions. Because, as we have argued, measures are fundamental to mathematics itself, our proposals are for work on numeracy rather than measures alone, but they are drawn either from the present project's findings, or from the notable absences in our report – that is, they are all directly relevant to measures.

9.1 Teaching and learning resources and pedagogy

We hope that the resources we developed, available copyright-free on the website, will be useful for practitioners and students. These materials are not presented as a new 'kit' for classroom teaching, but as examples of the kinds of work we propose. The range of teaching and learning materials available for numeracy teachers and students remains very limited; we need to explore both the development of more materials to be generally available, and ways for students and teachers to develop materials and projects appropriate to particular students and groups. The materials are designed to support group work (as distinct from both individual work and 'whole-class teaching'), itself an area which warrants further study and development. They are designed to enable adults with limited experience of formal measurement outside the classroom to expand their repertoire in supportive conditions; the materials provide 'jumping off points' for further exploration and learning.

We propose that such development take place alongside a review of the standards and the curriculum – both the ANCC itself, and the ways in which it is taught.

9.2 Curriculum review

When the curriculum is redrafted, the following points should be borne in mind. First, the notion of numeracy embodied in the curriculum fits only very poorly with what we know of the development and uses of mathematics skills and knowledge. A review of the ANCC should address fundamental questions of the nature of the relationships between skills, contexts, needs, interests, economic development and the development of mathematics itself. The present curriculum is founded on a view of mathematics as a hierarchy, translated into an order in which skills are to be developed. We suggest that if contexts and skills are derived from the mathematics in students' lives or the use of measures in wider society, a different conception would emerge.

Secondly, the present notion of levels, which has enormous importance in the organisation of classes, schemes of work and examinations does not reflect people's uses of numeracy skills.

Thirdly, the question of how numeracy, literacy, ESOL and ICT are linked, both conceptually and in student referral and placement, is important to the curriculum itself and to teaching, the development of materials, and the need for wider resources, including both equipment and links between staff. Although we worked only in numeracy classrooms, there is ample evidence in this report of the importance of considering issues of language and literacy alongside numeracy. Language and literacy issues might be important in any study of teaching and learning with a broadly Vygotskyan perspective, whatever the subject (chemistry, say, or citizenship). We highlight them here for two reasons: the language of measures and the place of numeracy in students' studies. The language of measures is particularly complex, with rich metaphorical uses and much ambiguity as well as precision, and yet there is little discussion of how students come to use terms with the exact meanings required in mathematical discourse. Almost all the students with whom we worked were also taking literacy and/or English for speakers of other languages, and many took ICT courses. Without agreeing that numeracy is a sub-set of literacy skills (cf. the IALS survey, e.g. OECD 1995; 1997), opportunities for students and teachers to work in a more integrated way across literacy, language and numeracy should be explored. For example, project work could be shared across all the strands of *Return to Study* or prison courses. (Associating literacy, numeracy and/or language classes under a 'Return to Learning' umbrella does not of itself link students' study across these areas.)

9.3 Expanding and developing provision

Further work is needed on course organisation and on the ways in which students are recruited and courses are negotiated around students' interests, skills and purposes.

In a small study, we have found examples of students working at inappropriate levels, with a mix of effects. Some students suffer further alienation from mathematics when work is too difficult and felt to be irrelevant; others are apparently recorded as 'achieving', in the terms of *Skills for Life*, when it is unclear that the tests are evidence of new learning. Questions of 'motivation', whether meaning students' purposes for studying numeracy or encouraging people to take up courses, warrant further study, and should be linked to the revision of the curriculum proposed above.

9.4 Numeracy embedded in other contexts

Our study was small, and worked only in 'generic' numeracy classrooms, that is, those where numeracy is the main topic to be studied. We have discussed in this report the importance of context for the meaning of measures (though the same is true for number, shape and space and handling data – cf. Coben (2003)). More work is needed to examine how the curriculum is or could be used in particular workplace training programmes. There is a developing body of work (much of it accessible through *Adults Learning Mathematics – an international research forum*, www.alm-online.org) on how mathematics is used in the workplace, on which research on numeracy education for the workplace could draw, and there are examples from elsewhere of the embedding of mathematics in workplace numeracy education. For example, Fownes, Thompson and Evetts (2002), commissioned by the construction industry, produced learning materials which relate a more theoretical understanding of mathematics to the skills required in particular workplaces.

9.5 Teachers' working lives and research

If teachers are to work in self-critical, research-based ways, more time must be found for them to reflect individually and collectively on their work and develop new approaches. The paucity of prior research makes it particularly important that not only the few teacher-researchers, but the numeracy teacher workforce as a whole have time to develop our work. As changes in teacher education gather pace, we should beware focusing solely on initial and postgraduate teacher education; a reduction in contact hours would support less formal continuing professional development.

9.6 Students' perspectives

The NRDC's review of research (Coben et al. 2003) noted the value of and need for students' research as well as teachers' and academic research. At the heart of the developments in numeracy associated with *Skills for Life* is an urgent sense from policy-makers that we (nationally) must change our stance towards numeracy. The number of people potentially involved is huge; we should see all students as experts in their own learning, with ways into discussions with other students which are impossible for teachers or researchers to match.

9.7 Summary

In this final section we have attempted to draw out the implications of our study for practice, policy and research. Our six broad suggestions are for work on numeracy as a whole rather than measures alone. We highlight, first, the need to explore both the development of more materials and ways for students and teachers to develop materials and projects appropriate to particular students and groups (group work being an area which itself warrants further study and development); such development should take place alongside a review of the standards and the curriculum. Secondly, a review of the ANCC should address fundamental questions of the nature of the relationships between skills, contexts, levels of work, interests, economic development and the development of mathematics itself, the nature of links between numeracy, literacy, ESOL and ICT, and the need for wider resources, including both equipment and links between staff. Thirdly, further work is needed on course organisation, student recruitment and course negotiation. Fourthly, more work is needed to examine how the curriculum is or could be used in particular workplace training programmes. Fifthly, teachers need more time to reflect individually and collectively on their work and to develop new approaches. Sixthly and finally, students should no longer be seen as lacking in motivation (or in need of encouragement) to make good their deficit in numeracy learning. Instead we should recognise students as experts in their own learning, listen to what they have to say and acknowledge that they can communicate with each other in ways unmatched by teachers or researchers. The materials produced as part of the project, suitably adapted, should enrich the experience of adult students – both those with limited experience of formal measurement outside the classroom and those whose experience and expertise outstrip the present adult numeracy core curriculum.

References

Abbott, A. (2002). 'Maths and Measurement: Developing measurement skills in adult learners of mathematics'. In L. Ø. Johansen & T. Wedege (Eds.), Numeracy for Empowerment and Democracy? Proceedings of the 8th International Conference of Adult Learning Mathematics – A Research Forum (ALM8) (pp. 44–49). Roskilde, Denmark: Centre for Research in Learning Mathematics, Roskilde University, in association with Adults Learning Mathematics – A Research Forum.

ABSSU. (2003). **'Get On' campaign**. Retrieved July 22 , 2003, from the world wide web: http://www.dfes.gov.uk/get-on/coursepro.shtml

Adams, T. L., & Harrell, G. (2003). Estimation at work. In D. H. Clements & G. Bright (Eds.), **Learning and teaching measurement: 2003 yearbook** (pp. 229–243). Reston, Virginia, USA: The National Council of Teachers of Mathematics, Inc.

Allen, J. (2004, April 4). **Bull's-eye in the numbers game: how the government is using a darts star to throw light on innumeracy**. The Guardian. Retrieved April 6, 2004, from the World Wide Web: http://education.guardian.co.uk/egweekly/story/0,5500,1186067,00.html

Barton, D. and Papen, U. (2005). **Linking literacy and numeracy programmes in developing countries and the UK**. London: NRDC.

Baxter, M. (2003). "More questions than answers". **Adults Learning**, 15(2), 27.

Baxter, M., Leddy, E., Richards, L., Tomlin, A., & Wresniwiro, T. (2004). Workshop on the Measures project. Göteborg, Sweden: Adults Learning Mathematics – 11 (unpublished conference presentation).

Baxter, M., Leddy, E., Richards, L., Wresniwiro, T., Tomlin, A., & Coben, D. (2003). 'Where is the mathematics in measurement?' In J. Maaß & W. Schlöglmann (Eds.), Learning Mathematics to Live and Work in our World. Proceedings of the 10th international conference on Adults Learning Mathematics (pp. 176–182). Strobl, Austria: Universitätsverlag Rudolf Trauner.

BERA. (2000, July 26th). **BERA (British Educational Research Association) Ethical Guidelines**. BERA. Retrieved 11 December, 2002, from the world wide web: http://www.bera.ac.uk/guidelines.html

Bishop, A. (1988). "Mathematics Education in its Cultural Context". **Educational Studies in Mathematics**, 19, 179–191.

Burkhardt, H. (1977). **Seven sevens are fifty? Mathematics for the real world**. Nottingham: Shell Centre for Mathematical Education.

Carraher, T. N. (1986). "From drawings to buildings: Working with mathematical scales". **International Journal of Behavioural Development**, 9, 527–544.

City & Guilds. (2003). **3792 Adult numeracy and adult literacy scheme documents. entry level 3 education & training: on the job – construction** [CD-Rom]. London: City & Guilds. Retrieved, 13 December 2004 from the World Wide Web.

Clements, D. H. (1999). "Teaching length measurement: research challenges". **School Science and Mathematics**, 99, 5–11.

Coben, D., & Thumpston, G. (1996). 'Common sense, good sense and invisible mathematics'. In T. Kjærgård, A. Kvamme & N. Lindén (Eds.), PDME III Proceedings: Numeracy, Gender, Class, Race, Proceedings of the Third International Conference of Political Dimensions of Mathematics Education (PDME) III, Bergen, Norway, July 24–27 1995 (pp. 284–298). Landås, Norway: Caspar.

Coben, D. (2001). 'Fact, fiction and moral panic: the changing adult numeracy curriculum in England.' In G. E. FitzSimons, J. O'Donoghue & D. Coben (Eds.), Adult and Life-long Education in Mathematics: Papers from Working Group for Action 6, 9th International Congress on Mathematical Education, ICME 9 (pp. 125–153). Melbourne: Language Australia in association with Adults Learning Mathematics – A Research Forum (ALM).

Coben, D., contributions by D. Colwell, S. Macrae, J. Boaler, M. Brown & V. Rhodes (2003). **Adult numeracy: review of research and related literature**. London: NRDC.

Coben, D., Leddy, E., Holder, D., Baker, E., Swain, J., & Tomlin, A. (2004). 'Exploring the moorland: teacher research into adult numeracy'. In D. Coben (Ed.), What counts as evidence for what purposes in adult literacy, numeracy and ESOL? Papers from the first NRDC international conference. (pp. 128–135). Nottingham: University of Nottingham and NRDC.

Coben, D. (2005). **Adult numeracy: shifting the focus. A report and recommendations on adult numeracy in Scotland**. Edinburgh: Learning Connections Scotland, Scottish Executive.

Cockcroft, W. H. (1982). **Mathematics counts: report of the committee of inquiry into the teaching of mathematics in schools**. HMSO: London.

D'Ambrosio, U. (1997) Ethnomathematics and its place in the history and pedagogy of mathematics. In A. Powell & M. Frankenstein (Eds.), **Ethnomathematics: challenging eurocentrism in mathematics education** (pp. 13–24). New York: Suny Press.

Davis, P. J., & Hersh, R. (1981). **The mathematical experience**. London: Penguin Books.

de Agüero, M. (2003). 'Studying mathematical everyday working problems.' Paper presented at the Adults Learning Mathematics – 10: Learning Mathematics to Live and Work in our World, Strobl, Austria.

DfES. (2001). **Skills for Life: the national strategy for improving adult literacy and numeracy skills**. DfEE/DfES. Retrieved, from the world wide web: www.dfes.gov.uk/readwriteplus

DfES. (2003, 30 Oct.). **The Skills for Life survey: a national needs and impact survey of literacy, numeracy and ICT skills**. Department for Education and Skills. Retrieved 12 Dec, 2003, from the World Wide Web: http://www.dfes.gov.uk/research/data/uploadfiles/RR490.pdf

DfES & Basic Skills Agency. (2001a). **Adult numeracy core curriculum**. Basic Skills Agency. Retrieved 1 September, 2003, from the World Wide Web: http://www.basic-skills.co.uk

DfES & Basic Skills Agency. (2001b). **An introduction to the adult numeracy core curriculum**. London: Basic Skills Agency.

Earle, L., Watson, N., & others. (2003). **Watching and learning 3. Final report of the external evaluation of England's national lteracy and numeracy strategies**. Ontario: Ontario Institute for Studies in Education, University of Toronto.

Eisenhart, M. A. (1988). "The ethnographic research tradition and mathematics education Research." **Journal for Research in Mathematics Education**, 19(2), 99–114.

Engl, H. (2003, 29 June). 'Mathematics and industry: A relationship for mutual benefit.' Paper presented at the Adults Learning Mathematics – 10: Learning Mathematics to Live and Work in our World, Strobl, Austria.

Ernest, P. (1998). **Social constructivism as a philosophy of mathematics**. New York: State University of New York Press.

Fauvel, J., & Gray, J. (Eds.). (1987). **The history of mathematics: a reader**. Basingstoke, UK: Macmillan Press/The Open University.

FitzSimons, G. E. (2000). "Lifelong learning: practice and possibility in the pharmaceutical industry." **Education and Training**, 42(3), 170–181.

FitzSimons, G. E., & Godden, G. L. (2000). Review of research on adults learning mathematics. In D. Coben, J. O'Donoghue & G. E. FitzSimons (Eds.), Perspectives on Adults Learning Mathematics (pp. 13 – 45). Dordrecht/Boston/London: Kluwer Academic Publishers.

Fownes, L., Thompson, E., & Evetts, J. (Eds.). (2002). **Numeracy at work**. Burnaby, BC, Canada: Skillplan (BC Construction Industry Skills Improvement Council).

Gall, M. G., Borg, W. R., & Gall, J. P. (1966) **Educational research: an introduction**. (6th ed.) White Plains, NY: Longman.

Gardener, S. (1992). **The long word club: the development of written language within adult fresh start and return to learning programmes**. Bradford: RaPAL.

Geddie, W. (Ed.). (1964). **Chambers' twentieth century dictionary**. Edinburgh and London: W. & R. Chambers.

Gerdes, P. (1997). On Culture, Geometrical Thinking and Mathematics Education. In A. Powell & M. Frankenstein (Eds.), **Ethnomathematics: challenging eurocentrism in mathematics education** (pp. 223–247). New York: Suny Press.

Gerdes, P. (1986). "How to recognize hidden geometrical thinking: A contribution to the development of anthropological mathematics." **For the Learning of Mathematics** 6(2): 10–17.

Gillespie, J. (2004). 'The 'Skills for Life' national survey of adult numeracy in England. What does it tell us? What further questions does it prompt?' 10th International Congress on Mathematical Education (ICME-10). Retrieved 12 January 2005 from the World Wide Web: http://www.icme-10.dk

Goodwin, J. (2004). 'Context and assessment items.' Paper presented at the Mathematics Education Research Group, King's College London.

Green, J., & Bloome, D. (1997). Ethnography and ethnographers of and in education: a situated perspective. In J. Flood, S. B. Heath & D. Lapp (Eds.), **Handbook of research on teaching literacy through the communicative and visual arts** (pp. 181–202). New York: International Reading Association and Macmillan Library Reference.

Gustafsson, L., & Mouwitz, L. (2004). **Adults and mathematics – a vital subject**. Göteborg, Sweden: NCM.

Harris, M. (1997) **Common threads: women, mathematics and work**. Stoke on Trent: Trentham Books.

Hebra, A. (2003). **Measure for measure: the story of imperial, metric and other units**. Baltimore and London: The Johns Hopkins Press.

Hillier, Y., & Jameson, J. (2003). **Empowering researchers in further education**. Stoke on Trent: Trentham Books.

Hoyles, C., Noss, R., & Pozzi, S. (2001). "Proportional reasoning in nursing practice." **Journal for Research in Mathematics Education**, 32(1), 4–27.

Johnston, B. (2002). 'Calculating people: measurement as a social process'. In L. Ø. Johansen & T. Wedege (Eds.), Numeracy for Empowerment and Democracy? Proceedings of the 8th International Conference of Adults Learning Mathematics - A Research Forum (ALM8) (pp. 112-119). Roskilde, Denmark: Centre for Research in Learning Mathematics, Roskilde University, in association with Adults Learning Mathematics - A Research Forum

Johnston, B., Baynham, M., Kelly, S., Barlow, K., & Marks, G. (1997). **Numeracy in practice: effective pedagogy in numeracy for unemployed young people**. Sydney: Centre for Language and Literacy, University of Technology, Sydney & Dept. of Employment, Training and Youth Affairs.

Joseph, G. G. (1991). **The crest of the peacock: non-european roots of mathematics**. London: I. B. Taurus and Co.

Kress, G. (2000). "The Futures of Literacy." **RaPAL Bulletin**, 42.

Lave, J. (1988). **Cognition in practice: mind, mathematics and culture in everyday life**. Cambridge: Cambridge University Press.

Lave, J. (1992). Word problems: A microcosm of theories of learning. In P. Light & G. Butterworth (Eds.), **Context and cognition: ways of learning and knowing**. (pp. 74–92). New York: Harvester Wheatsheaf.

Learning Connections Adult Literacies Team. (2003). **Adult Literacies in Scotland**. Retrieved 23 Aug., 2004, from the world wide web: http://communitiesscotland.gov.uk/Web/Site/cl/al_main.asp

Leddy, E. (2004). 'Why I became a teacher researcher'. Notes for an NRDC teacher researcher conference. London: Birkbeck College, 30 January.

Lerman, S. (1990). 'Mathematics education and the new 'Dependency Culture'.' In R. Noss, A. Brown, P. Dowling, P. Drake, M. Harris, C. Hoyles & S. Mellin-Olson (Eds.), Political Dimensions of Mathematics Education: action and critique. Proceedings of the first international conference (Revised ed., pp. 153–160). London: Institute of Education, University of London.

Linchevski, L., & Kutscher, B. (1998). "Tell me with whom you are learning, and I'll tell you how much you have learned: mixed-ability grouping in mathematics". **Journal for Research in Mathematics Education**, 29(5), 533–544.

Lincoln, Y. S., and Guba, E. G. **Naturalistic inquiry.** Thousand Oaks, CA: Sage, 1985.

Lindenskov, L. (2003). 'Teachers' approaches to mathematics to live and work – a model of four stages'. In J. Maasz & W. Schloeglmann (Eds.), Learning Mathematics to Live and Work in our World. Proceedings of the 10th international conference of Adults Learning Mathematics (pp. 146–153). Strobl, Austria: Universitätsverlag Rudolf Trauner.

Llorente, J. C. (2000). Researching adults' knowledge through Piagetian clinical exploration – the case of domestic work. In D. Coben, J. O'Donoghue & G. E. FitzSimons (Eds.), **Perspectives on adults learning mathematics: research and practice** (pp. 67–81). Dordrecht, The Netherlands: Kluwer Academic Publishers.

Lumpkin, B. (1997). Africa in the Mainstream of Mathematics History. In A. Powell & M. Frankenstein (Eds.), **Ethnomathematics: challenging eurocentrism in Mathematics Education** (pp. 101–117). New York: Suny Press.

Mace, J. (1998). **Playing with time: mothers and the meaning of literacy**. London: UCL Press Ltd.

McClain, K., Cobb, P., Gravemeijer, K. & Estes, B. (1999) V. L. Stiff & R. F. Curcia (Eds), **Developing mathematical reasoning in grades K-12, 1999 yearbook**. Reston, VA: National Council of Teachers of Mathematics. Retrieved 12 January 2005 from the World Wide Web, http://www.wcer.wisc.edu/ncisla/publications/

Merriam, S. B. (1998) **Qualitative research and case study applications in education**. San Francisco, CA: Jossey-Bass Publishers.

Milroy, W. (1992). An ethnographic study of the mathematical ideas of a group of carpenters. **Journal for Research in Mathematics Education** Monograph 5. Reston, VA, USA: National Council of Teachers of Mathematics.

Moll, L. C., & Greenberg, J. B. (1992). Creating zones of possibilities: Combining social contexts for instruction. In L. C. Moll (Ed.), **Vygotsky and education: instructional implications and applications of sociohistorical psychology** (pp. 319 – 348). Cambridge: Cambridge University Press.

Noss, R. (1997) **New cultures, new numeracies**. London: Institute of Education, University of London

Nuñes, T., Light, P., & Mason, J. (1993). "Tools for thought: the measurement of length and area". **Learning and Instruction**, 3(1), 39–54.

Nuñes, T., & Moreno, C. (2000, October). **An intervention programme for promoting deaf pupils' achievement in mathematics**. Oxford Brookes University. Retrieved 23 August, 2004, from the World Wide Web: http://www.brookes.ac.uk/schools/social/psych/staff/deafedu/programme.html!

Nuñes, T., Schliemann, A. D., & Carraher, D. W. (1993). **Street mathematics and school mathematics**. Cambridge: Cambridge University Press.

OECD. (1995). **Literacy, economy and society. Results of the first International Adults Literacy Survey**. Canada: Statistics Canada.

OECD, Human Resources Development Canada & Minister of Industry Canada (1997). **Literacy skills for the knowledge society. Further results from the International Adult Literacy Survey**. Paris: Organisation for Economic Co-operation and Development.

Patrick, R. (1999). "Not your usual maths course: Critical mathematics education for adults". **Higher Education Research and Development**, 18(1), 85–98.

Pickard, P., & Alexander, P. (2001). 'The effects of digital measuring equipment on the concept of number'. In M. J. Schmitt & K. Safford-Ramus (Eds.), A Conversation between Researchers and Practitioners. Adults Learning Mathematics – 7. Proceedings of ALM-7 the Seventh International Conference of Adults Learning Mathematics – A Research Forum (pp. 141–146). Cambridge, MA: National Center for the Study of Adult Learning and Literacy (NCSALL), Harvard University Graduate School of Education, in association with Adults Learning Mathematics – A Research Forum (ALM).

Prisoners' [later Offenders'] Learning and Skills Unit (DfES). (2003). **Prisoners' learning and skills unit: FAQs** [web page]. DfES. Retrieved 22 July, 2003, from the World Wide Web: http://www.dfes.gov.uk/prisonerlearning/faqs.cfm

QCA (2001) **National standards for adult literacy and numeracy**. London: Qualifications and Curriculum Authority.

Robson, C. (1993) **Real world research: a resource for social scientists and practitioner-researchers**. London: Blackwell.

Scottish Executive. (2003). **Adult literacy and numeracy in Scotland**. Retrieved 23 Aug., 2004, from the World Wide Web: http://www.scotland.gov.uk/library3/lifelong/alan-03.asp#32

Sfard, A., Nesher, P., Streefland, L., Cobb, P., & Mason, J. (1998). "Learning Mathematics through Conversation: Is It as Good as They Say?" **For the Learning of Mathematics**, 18(1), 41–51.

Skovsmose, O. (1994). **Towards a philosophy of critical mathematics education**. Dordrecht; London: Kluwer Academic Publishers.

Sommerlad, E. (2003). "Theory, research and practice – the problematic appearance of 'pedagogy' in post-compulsory education". **Journal of Adult and Continuing Education**, 8(3), 147–164.

Steinback, M., Schmitt, M. J., Merson, M., & Leonelli, E. (2003). Measurement in adult education: Starting with students' understandings. In D. H. Clements & G. Bright (Eds.), **Learning and teaching measurement: 2003 yearbook** (pp. 304–317). Reston, Virginia, USA: The National Council of Teachers of Mathematics, Inc.

Stephan, M., Bowers, J., & et al (2003). **Supporting students' development of measuring conceptions: analyzing students' learning in social context**. Reston, VA: National Council for Teachers of Mathematics.

Sträßer, R. (2003). 'Mathematics at work: adults and artefacts.' In J. Maasz & W. Schloeglmann (Eds.), Learning mathematics to live and work in our world: Proceedings of the 10th international conference on Adults Learning Mathematics (pp. 30 – 37). Linz, Austria: Universitätsverlag Rudolf Trauner.

Tomlin, A. (2001). **Participatory approaches to work with adult basic mathematics students**. Unpublished PHD thesis, King's College London, London.

Tomlin, A. (2002a). "Literacy approaches in the numeracy classroom". **Literacy and Numeracy Studies**, 11(2), 9–24.

Tomlin, A. (2002b). "Real life' in everyday and academic maths.' In P. Valero & O. Skovsmose (Eds.), Proceedings of the Mathematics, Education and Society Conference (MES3), 2nd – 7th April 2002, *Helsingør, Denmark* (Vol. 2, pp. 471–479). Roskilde, Denmark: Centre for Research in Learning Mathematics, Danish University of Education.

Tout, D. (1997). Adults learning mathematics in context: some reflections on adult numeracy. In D. Coben (Ed.), **Adults learning mathematics – 3** (pp. 13–15). London: Goldsmiths College, University of London and ALM.

van Groenestijn, M. (2003). 'Functional numeracy'. In J. Maasz & W. Schloeglmann (Eds.), Learning mathematics to live and work in our world: Proceedings of the 10th international conference on Adults Learning Mathematics (pp. 9–18). Linz, Austria: Universitätsverlag Rudolf Trauner.

Yarnit, M. (1995). Piecing together the fragments: thoughts on adult education in a vanished era. In M. Mayo & J. Thompson (Eds.), **Adult learning, critical intelligence and social change** (pp. 69–81). Leicester: National Institute of Adult Continuing Education.

Zevenbergen, R. & Zevenbergen, K. (2004). 'The numeracies of boat building.' Paper presented at Topic Study Group 7, ICME-10, Copenhagen, Denmark. Retrieved 12 January 2005 from the World Wide Web at http://www.icme-organisers.dk/tsg07/ZEVENBERGEN.pdf

Appendix 1

Invitation to students to join measures project

Slide 2

During your classes

The tutor will be finding out as much as possible about what happens when people are working on measurement. It may include …

- taping all or part of a lesson
- making copies of students' work
- making very detailed notes about the class
- trying out new materials or activities

The tapes, notes or copies of work are called 'data'.

The tutor will share some of the data with other members of the research team, so we build up a picture of what is happening in your class. We will compare all the classes to each other and look for patterns:

- what helps people to improve their measurement skills?
- are some materials or activities better than others?
- do people learn more quickly if they work together, or is individual work best?
- do the same ways of working help all the students, or do people learn differently from each other?

We will be developing some new learning materials, which we hope students will try out. Your comments will help us improve the materials.

Slide 1

An invitation to join a research project

Learning and teaching measurement

What helps people improve their measurement skills?

This new research project will take place during your usual classes, and we may also ask to interview you.

What do I have to do?

You can take part in as much or as little of the research as you like. These are some examples:

- you agree to the tutor using notes about your work in the class, but you may decide not to be interviewed
- there may be a group of students who would like a discussion on a particular topic
- you may start being fully involved in the research and then decide to drop out of the project
- you may be fully involved in the research all the way through.

All tutors take notes, whether or not there is a research project. If you do not want take part in the research project, the notes about you will not be shown to the research team.

Your rights

- We will not use any data about you without your permission.
- You will be able to check any quotation before we use it.
- You may leave the research project at any time.
- The research is independent of your classes. You will not be penalised by the college or the tutor if you do not join the research project.
- All the students in the research will have pseudonyms. You can choose a name for yourself, or we will give you one.

This research project is funded by the government through the *National Research and Development Centre for Adult Literacy and Numeracy* (NRDC). The NRDC is researching ways of teaching and learning literacy, numeracy and ESOL (English for Speakers of Other Languages).

For more information, contact your tutor, or Alison Tomlin, King's College London. Telephone 020 7848 3945, email alison.tomlin@kcl.ac.uk

3

Interviews

We would like to interview some students about their experiences of working on measurement. We will ask questions like these:

- what are your aims in mathematics education?
- when and what do you need to measure? How do you do it at the moment?
- what do you think is the best way of improving your skills?
- what do you think of the classroom materials or activities?
- how could we improve the way we teach and learn measurement?
- how does measurement fit in with the rest of what you want to learn?
- how do you know if you are making progress?
- is what you learn really useful to you?

You are the only person who really knows what works for you. You know whether you feel more or less confident about your skills and which ways of learning suit you. We need your experience and advice.

Who will know about the research?

We will be talking about the research at conferences, tutors' training courses and staff meetings. We will write articles for journals, and some reports will be on the website. At the end of the project we will produce learning materials and we hope they will go to adult education courses across the country.

3

Appendix 2

Invitation to students to plan a workshop on measurement

The story so far .....

We have been working on a research project to find better ways of working on measurement.

Ideas and questions

Why work on measurement?

Many students don't need measurement skills in their day to day lives, but they want to help their children, or take an exam. For others, it's important in practical jobs, and for some people it's important at work. How can we make measurement lessons more interesting?

Some students have difficulties with **decimal numbers** - for example, changing 50 centimetres to 0.5 metres.

The **language** of measurement is difficult. Is the length always the longest side? Why do width, breadth and depth sometimes mean the same thing? Often there isn't a clear answer – but students need to be familiar with the terms and how they may be used.

Why is **time** often easier than weight, volume and length?

People don't agree about the best **way of working**. Practical activities, or worksheets? Quiet concentration, or a lot of discussion? Alone, in a small group or the whole class together? Should classes always be led by the teacher, or is some student-only time helpful?

Learning and teaching measurement

An invitation

to plan a workshop

for numeracy students

For more information, contact your tutor, or
Alison Tomlin, DEPS,
King's College London, Franklin Wilkins Building,
Stamford St, London SE1 9NN
Tel. 020 7848 3945, email alison.tomlin@kcl.ac.uk

Why do we want a students' workshop on measurement?

We have been working on the project for a year. We want to try out some new materials and teaching approaches, and see what students think of them. We hope to have the workshop in the spring or early summer.

Could you help
with planning the students' workshop?

We need to find a suitable venue, agree a budget, fix the date, advertise the workshop ... and you may be able to help with those.

But above all, we need to plan the workshop itself. We need students' ideas to help us make the event a success. If you have any views about what might make the workshop go well, then we need you!

We can pay your travel expenses to the planning meeting, and we will try to arrange it at a time and place that suits everyone.

If you might be able to help, please give the form to your tutor, or post it to Alison Tomlin, or email/telephone Alison (details overleaf).

What happens next?

Alison will contact you to find a convenient time and venue for the first planning meeting.

Thank you from the research team: Mark Baxter, Eamonn Leddy, Liz Richards, Topo Wresniwiro and Alison Tomlin.

Name ....

College or education centre..

How can we contact you? Please give your address, telephone number, email address or tutor's name

....

....

....

Comments, if any: ....

....

....

....

National Research and Development Centre
for adult literacy and numeracy

Appendix 3

Invitation to the seminar on measurement

Slide 2

We are doing some activities to make it easy and interesting to do some measurement, and we want your help and advice. It is part of a research project on adult numeracy courses. Anybody interested, come along and bring your ideas with you!

For more information, contact your tutor,

or

Alison Tomlin, DEPS,
King's College London, Franklin Wilkins Building,
Stamford St, London SE1 9NN
Tel. 020 7848 3945, e-mail alison.tomlin@kcl.ac.uk

Slide 1

Adult students' seminar on measurement

Are you returning to study and working on numeracy?

The students of Westminster Kingsway would like to invite other adult students to a seminar on measurement:

**Tuesday, 30 March,
10 am – 12.30 pm**

at Westminster Kingsway College,
Battersea Park Road, London SW11

3

NRDC
National Research and Development Centre
for adult literacy and numeracy

Please send this form to Alison Tomlin (address overleaf)

Name..

College or education centre ....
....

How can we contact you? Please give your address,
telephone number, email address or tutor's name
....
....
....

Transport and crèche requirements, and any other
comments: ....
....
....

3

Transport

We can help with the cost of
transport - for example, we
can pay for a minicab shared
by students.

Refreshments

Crèche

You can bring children
(over 2 years old)
to the crèche
but please book first.

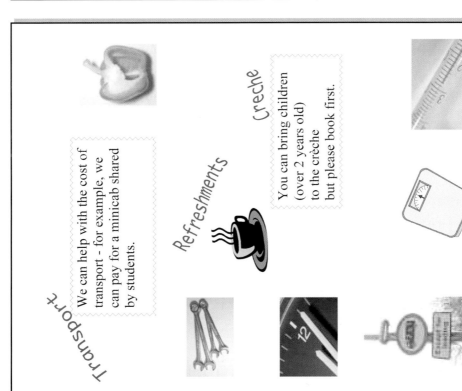

Appendix 4

Taking a wider view: teaching, learning, teacher research and the measures project

In section 3 we outlined research on the use, teaching and learning of measures. Here we take a wider view, first surveying theories of teaching and learning generally and then their application to mathematics, and relating them to our own project. We then consider the status of teacher research.

1   Teaching and learning: a 'social turn'

In line with a 'social turn' in the psychology of mathematics education we see teaching and learning in mathematics and numeracy classrooms as fundamentally social in nature, and mathematics itself as a set of cultural tools (Lerman, 2000). We have taken a broadly Vygotskyan view of teaching and learning (FitzSimons, 2002, 2003; Lerman, 1998; Moll, 1992); for overviews in adult learning and numeracy respectively, see Tusting and Barton (2003) and Coben et al. (2003). We have used ethnographic research tools (Green & Bloome, 1997) and our data analysis methods are consistent with those of grounded theory (Eisenhart, 1988; Hillier & Jameson, 2003). We used QSR Nud*ist software, coding both for categories emerging from the data and for curriculum elements.

Our project was not focused on developing theory, but here we seek briefly to situate the project in a wider perspective, based on a review by Elizabeth Sommerlad of the meanings of pedagogy across post-compulsory education. We use our discussion of key issues to point to questions about our own research.

Sommerlad astutely identifies a danger for our project:

> *A theory of pedagogy, as distinct from a theory of learning, must encompass all the complex factors that influence the process of teaching and learning. The lack of good pedagogic models and frameworks tends to leave researchers and practitioners without strong anchorage for concepts drawn from diverse literatures.* (Sommerlad, 2003: 157)

Sommerlad and her colleagues looked for pedagogic models that had received wide empirical confirmation in a variety of settings; they found instead a 'wealth of small-scale, mainly descriptive or modestly analytic studies and accounts of classroom practice' which 'distil the practical wisdom of able teaching staff' (Sommerlad, 2003: 151). Many looked at outcomes and attainments; few looked at connections with pedagogy, so that 'a coherent intellectualised view of pedagogy is still lacking' (ibid.).

Sommerlad summarises core concepts in 'new wave' learning theories, many of them referencing Vygotsky:

■ an emphasis on learning as a social or distributed activity rather than an individual cognitive activity;

- a focus on learning in communities rather than as isolated individuals;
- incorporation of the social world of the learner into the educator's identity; and
- the centrality of the learning setting or context to the learning process. (op.cit.: 152).

There is a mismatch between this list and the stated and implied assumptions of the ANCC. Although the training has emphasised particular forms of group work and whole class teaching (DfES & Basic Skills Agency, 2001b), the individual, decontextualised testing regime stands in contradiction to these ideas of pedagogy. Further, small group work might be supposed to be designed to facilitate students' co-teaching but we have found no sources for a theory of learning underlying the curriculum and training.

Sommerlad cites Malcolm and Zukas (2000; 2001), who use the notion of communities of practice as a conceptual tool for mapping the literature; they identify a continuing preoccupation with the individual learner. In adult numeracy we have a contradiction: the curriculum claims to focus on the individual learner (via the ILP) but the individual may be over-ridden and become fodder for target practice (as we saw in the case of HMP Brixton). Further, although the learner 'brings' her/his context (DfES & Basic Skills Agency, 2001a), the mathematics/numeracy itself stands free of context, that is, free of any notion of either individual or community (we address the question of the relationship of mathematics to context in sections 3, 6 and 9). This is consistent with Sommerlad's comment:

> In [some] areas of adult and community education, there are strong pressures for accountability and measurement of outcomes in conformity with government targets for attainment, which is reflected in a shift away from andragogic principles to a narrower set of pedagogic practices. (op.cit.: 153)

'Andragogic' refers to adult as distinct from children's education. Sommerlad argues that within education, the recent change of discourse from 'education' (institutions and systems) to 'learning' implies a paradigm shift for policy makers and educationists: 'a letting go and a wider colonising simultaneously' (op.cit.: 149). This catches our own misgivings about the term 'learner' (discussed in section 9), which has become a required key word in adult education and adult education research, and bears little relationship to its meanings in non-research and non-policy circles. In all the centres in which the teacher-researchers worked the term student was used, by teachers and students alike, and we have kept their usage.

Sommerlad summarises the shifts involved in what Lerman (2000) calls the social turn in the psychology of education:

- atomistic-empiricist theories (behaviourism and cognitivism) focus on behaviours
- functionalistic-developmental theories (constructivism) focus on the whole person
- contextual theories (humanism, situational, and cognitive theories) add the context of action and learning; and
- socio-historical-anthropological theories (activity, social reproduction, and participation theories) add the wider context: society, culture and history.

Each layer adds to the previous one, as research in post-compulsory education develops:

> Dominant traditions and practices remain well entrenched, but emergent theories are occupying the new space as 'learning' moves out from institutional settings into less formal and informal settings, and, in turn, are challenging key elements of the learning patrimony. (op. cit.: 156)

Educational research is moving from individualised psychological theories to a critical or socio-cultural approach, in which:

> *Learning is a contextually embedded process in which people learn skills in the context of their application to authentic problems. (op. cit.: 156)*

We described in section 6 work on measures using 'authentic problems', though by that we do not mean 'real world' problems, but problems which were interesting, engaging and had no obvious solution. Judging by students' assessments of their classroom experiences, work on the problems was very productive. However, learning materials or problems do not direct the processes of classroom life; that depends on the teacher and students, but particularly on the teacher, and on her/his relationship with the constraints of the systems within which s/he works. We note Sommerlad's caution:

> *We ... observed from the literature review a tendency for imported innovative practices to be 'neutered' or absorbed into the prevailing learning patrimony, losing their epistemological underpinning and critical edge. Problem-based learning and project-based learning are prone to this. (op. cit.: 157)*

Next we consider the relationship of classroom numeracy to students' numeracy practices outside formal education. Here we draw on the work of Luis Moll and Marta Civil, again working within Vygotskyan traditions.

We take a notion of 'funds of knowledge' from the work of Luis Moll and others working in a similar vein. Moll and Greenberg describe work with Mexican families in Tucson, seeking to analyse household activities in order to create reciprocal relations between households' practices and instruction in schools; we suggest the key concepts are transferable to a narrower focus on numeracy. Ethnographic methods uncovered

> *the social sharing of knowledge as part of the households' functioning, what we have labeled the exchange of 'funds of knowledge' ... These networks form social contexts for the transmission of knowledge, skills, and information, as well as cultural values and norms.* (Moll & Greenberg, 1992: 320-1)

Funds of knowledge can be understood, write Moll and Greenberg, in relation to other household funds, for example funds of rent (payable in money, produce or labour) or ceremonial funds:

> *Each of these funds ... entails a broader set of activities which require specific knowledge of strategic importance to households. These bodies of knowledge are what we call funds of knowledge ... It is unnecessary and unfeasible for individual persons or households to possess all this knowledge; when needed, such knowledge is available and accessible through social networks. [As well as traditional knowledge,] households ... share ... funds of knowledge specific to urban living, such as access to institutional assistance, school programs, transportation, occupational opportunities, and other services. In short, **households' funds of knowledge are wide-ranging and abundant**. (Op. cit.: 323)*

Funds of knowledge are manifested through events or activities; they are not possessions or traits of individuals, but 'characteristics of people-in-an-activity' (op. cit.: 326). They are available regardless of the families' years of formal schooling, yet rarely make their way into classrooms, and are an untapped resource for academic instruction. Further, without a focus on social relationships and persons-in-activities, 'it is very easy for outsiders (educators) to underestimate the wealth of funds of knowledge available in working-class households' (op. cit.: 327). The authors argue that by 'mobilising funds of knowledge' and connecting classrooms and outside resources, classrooms can become more advanced contexts for teaching and learning (op. cit.: 344).

In a series of papers Marta Civil (2000; 2001; 2002) extends and adapts Moll's notion of funds of knowledge to numeracy work with US Spanish-speaking parents. Initially established to help parents help their school children, the project found that the students wanted mathematics education for themselves too. Through using the parents' funds of knowledge combined with other sources, the students developed new, formal mathematics skills - that is, Civil's work provides an example of a link between the community's funds of knowledge and formal education. One such development is the parents' choice to work on algebra (Civil, 2001), as some students in our own project proposed (section 5).

The notion of funds of knowledge may help us understand people's confidence (discussed in section 5) in dealing with measures outside the classroom, often despite a lack of formal education in measures. Community funds of knowledge may explain why people seem, in general, not to feel a lack of numeracy skills but nevertheless to 'fail' in surveys and tests (cf. DfES, 2003; Gillespie, 2004, discussed below).

2   Teacher research

We have described our own methods, but here we address questions relating to teacher research overall. Where do we fit? Much of the literature on teacher research is concerned with the means and benefits of taking part in research for the teacher (cf. Brown & Dowling, 1998; Brown & Jones, 2001). Our focus however was not directly on the processes of the research, or on teacher researcher development, but on teaching and learning in a specific area of the curriculum.

Martha Merson introduces a collection of studies by Massachusetts adult literacy teacher-researchers:

> It is not our intent to reach an audience of academic education researchers with 'research findings' that would be acceptable to highly trained quantitative or qualitative researchers. We aim instead to reach teachers like ourselves who have questions about our practice that can best be answered by us: insiders in the classroom community. (Leonelli, Merson, Schmitt, & members of the Massachusetts ABE Math Team, 1994)

Why would any findings (though clearly Merson is nervous of the term) be unacceptable to researchers? Were the analyses not done thoroughly? Did the writers fail to deal with inconsistencies or contradictions in the data? Are reports written for researchers inappropriate for teachers, and vice versa? These may be the questions that readers ask of our own report. Most of the authors in Leonelli et al. combine accounts of classroom research with comments on changes in their own beliefs and practice; the effect is that the collection studies teachers' development as well as each teacher's particular research question. The book serves to introduce the issue we now raise. Much of the teacher research we have read is focused on the processes of research and its role in teacher development, rather than on the research questions and findings. What is the status of the findings of teacher research?

A group of literacy educators in Canada offer both summaries of research perspectives relevant to teacher research and teachers' accounts of their research (Pheasey et al., 2000); Mary Norton (Ch. 2, Pheasey et al., 2000) surveys the influences of John Dewey, humanistic education, critical pedagogy, and feminist pedagogies. Cochran-Smith and Lytle (1993) contrast research on teaching and teacher research. The latter is described as generally:

> *emerging from the problems of practice: felt discrepancies between intention and reality, theory/research and practice; [it is] reflexive and referenced to the immediate context. (op.cit.: 12)*

The findings of research on teaching are 'intended for application ... outside of the context in which they were developed', whereas the findings of teacher research are 'intended for application and use within the context in which they were developed' (ibid). The authors comment:

> *The criterion of generalizability has been used to discount the value of research prompted by the questions of individual teachers and conducted in single classrooms. (op.cit.: 13)*

In defence, they argue that understanding one classroom helps us to understand better all classrooms. What of our project? We do not claim that having more than one teacher-researcher of itself makes our findings more generalisable, but rather that sharing terrain helped us develop our ideas and gave us access to the views of a wider, but still limited, group of students. We can recognise the teacher-researchers' interest in the project as arising from 'felt discrepancies between intention and reality' in their teaching, insofar as all sought to improve their practice - but the starting point of the project was a government initiative, 'intended for application outside of the context in which [the findings] were developed'.

Cochran-Smith and Lytle argue that teacher research relies on:

> *a different epistemology that regards inquiry by teachers themselves as a distinctive and important way of knowing about teaching [...] What is worth knowing about teaching would include [...] what teachers, who are researchers in their own classrooms, can know through systematic subjectivity. Teacher researchers are uniquely positioned to provide a truly emic, or insider's, perspective that makes visible the ways that students and teachers together construct knowledge and curriculum. (op.cit.: 43)*

Knowledge will accumulate as communities of teachers and researchers read and critique each others' work, building a 'different kind of "interpretive universe"' (op.cit.: 59). We hope that our own study contributes to a body of teacher research which will develop further in future projects.

We turn now to a review by Bridget Somekh (2003) of developments in the theory of action research, with relevance for teacher research more generally. We have cited Vygotsky, but here we find his work characterised as a 'birdcage':

> *I do remember having a bit of trouble with applying Vygotsky, as ready-made theory, to action research. [I think it was] my antipathy to theorists trying to trap the complexities of action research into their limited theoretical birdcage. On balance, I prefer a much more creative, postmodern approach to developing action research theory. (Marian Dadds, quoted in Somekh, op. cit.: 249)*

Somekh reflects on her own experience in teacher education:

> *Interviewing students for the first time opened my eyes to the unintended consequences of teaching behaviours and revealed the rather obvious - but to me entirely unexpected - truth that students are experts on pedagogy, although they do not always understand the beliefs and theories that are driving teachers' practice. (op.cit.: 250)*

We argue that though students recognise good (or poor) pedagogy, that isn't same as being able to describe it; and whether there is such a thing as a universally 'good pedagogy' remains to be established. Further, in our own contexts we worked only with students who had stayed the course. There is little research with people who try and then reject numeracy education, or who simply pass it by.

Somekh provides an overview of the development of teacher research (focusing on work in Britain), with reference particularly to the influence of John Elliott (e.g. Elliott, 1991). She argues that the theory-practice relationship is interactive, and that external validity and therefore generalisability are demonstrated when insights are translated into an improved quality of action. So what will teachers make of our report? Will it lead to 'an improved quality of action'? Further, who will judge whether teaching and learning have improved – students, teachers, examination boards or government?

Before leaving methodology we briefly look at feminist standpoint theory, which starts from the position that socially oppressed people have knowledge, particularly of social relations, that is unavailable to the privileged. Sandra Harding argues:

> *All of the kinds of objectivity-maximizing procedures focused on the nature and/or social relations that are the direct object of observation and reflection must also be focused on the observers and reflectors, [that is,] scientists and the larger society whose assumptions they share. But a maximally critical study of scientists and their communities can be done only from the perspective of those whose lives have been marginalised by such communities. (Harding, 1993:69)*

Harding makes the case for a critical study from the perspective of, in our case, those who have been marginalised by education in the past: adult numeracy students, whom we can assume had a less than successful experience of school numeracy/mathematics education. That is not offered here: however closely we have listened to students, their views are accessed only through the team's questions and observations. We would argue for research by, as well as for and about, students: that remains a gap in adult numeracy research (Coben et al., 2003; Tomlin, 2001a, 2001b).

The *Measures* project does not fit well the descriptions of teacher research outlined here; we need further work on the epistemology and methodology of teacher research. We hope that this study, alongside other NRDC teacher research reports, will contribute to a more developed body of work. Compared to most of the teacher research studies we have read, our project was more substantial: a team of teacher-researchers working on shared research questions; more time for each teacher-researcher; and more researcher time. We addressed problems identified by teacher-researchers in their own practice, but the project was established not by the teacher-researchers but by a government-related organisation, with employer support, and its findings were intended to have much wide relevance. We do not claim generalisability but something looser: the relevance of the project for others may depend on the degree and transparency of critical reflexivity. Margaret Eisenhart (1988) notes that reliability is often poor in ethnographic studies; she advises researchers to give enough detail to enable other researchers to undertake similar studies, and we hope we have done so. We hope too that we have written in such a way that the project has what Patti Lather (1986) calls face validity - that is, research that is recognised as working by its readers, and triggers a 'yes of course' response.

References

Brown, A. J., & Dowling, P. C. (1998). **Doing research/reading research: a mode of interrogation for education**. London: Falmer.

Brown, T., & Jones, L. (2001). **Action research and postmodernism: congruence and critique**. Buckingham, UK and Philadelphia, USA: Open University Press.

City & Guilds. (2003). **3792 Adult Numeracy and Adult Literacy Scheme documents. Entry 3 Education & training: On the job - Construction** [CD-Rom]. London: City & Guilds.

Civil, M. (2000). 'Parents as Learners of Mathematics'. In S. Johnson & D. Coben (Eds.), ALM-6: Proceedings of the sixth international conference of Adults Learning Mathematics - a Research Conference (pp. 141-147). Nottingham: CEP, University of Nottingham, in association with Adults Learning Mathematics - A Research Forum (ALM).

Civil, M. (2001). 'Parents as learners and teachers of mathematics: Toward a Two-Way Dialogue'. In M. J. Schmitt & K. Safford-Ramus (Eds.), Adults Learning Mathematics -7: A conversation between researchers and practitioners (pp. 173-175). 2001: National Centre for the Study of Adult Learning and Literacy (NCSALL), Harvard University Graduate School of Education, in association with **Adults Learning Mathematics - a Research Forum** (ALM).

Civil, M. (2002). 'Mathematics for Parents: Issues of Pedagogy and Content.' In L. O. Johansen & T. Wedege (Eds.), Numeracy for empowerment and democracy? Proceedings of the 8th international conference on Adults Learning Mathematics (2001) (pp. 60-67). Roskilde University, Denmark: Centre for Research in Learning Mathematics in association with Adults Learning Mathematics - A Research Forum.

Coben, D., contributions by D. Colwell, Macrae, S., Boaler, J., M., B., & Rhodes, V. (2003). **Adult numeracy: review of research and related literature**. London: NRDC.

Cochran-Smith, M., & Lytle, S. L. (1993). **Inside Outside: Teacher Research and Knowledge**. New York: Teachers College Press.

DfES. (2003, 30 Oct.). **The Skills for Life survey: a national needs and impact survey of literacy, numeracy and ICT skills**. Department for Education and Science. Retrieved 12 Dec, 2003, from the World Wide Web: http://www.dfes.gov.uk/research/data/uploadfiles/RR490.pdf

DfES & Basic Skills Agency. (2001a). **Adult numeracy core curriculum**. Basic Skills Agency. Retrieved 1 September, 2003, from the World Wide Web: http://www.basic-skills.co.uk

DfES & Basic Skills Agency. (2001b). **An introduction to the Adult Numeracy Core Curriculum**. London: Basic Skills Agency.

Eisenhart, M. A. (1988). "The Ethnographic Research Tradition and Mathematics Education Research." **Journal for Research in Mathematics Education,** 19(2), 99-114.

Elliott, J. (1991). **Action Research for Educational Change**. Milton Keynes: Open University Press.

FitzSimons, G. E. (2002). **What counts as mathematics? Technologies of power in adult and vocational education**. Dordrecht, The Netherlands: Kluwer Academic Publishers.

FitzSimons, G. E. (2003). "Using Engeström's expansive learning framework to analyse a case study in adult mathematics education." **Literacy and Numeracy Studies,** 12(2), 47-63.

Gillespie, J. (2004). 'The 'Skills for Life' national survey of adult numeracy in England. What does it tell us? What further questions does it prompt?' 10th International Congress on Mathematical Education (ICME-10). Retrieved, from the World Wide Web: http://www.icme-10.dk

Green, J., & Bloome, D. (1997). Ethnography and ethnographers of and in education: a situated perspective. In J. Flood & S. B. Heath & D. Lapp (Eds.), **Handbook of research on teaching literacy through the communicative and visual arts** (pp. 181-202). New York: International Reading Association and Macmillan Library Reference.

Harding, S. (1993). Rethinking standpoint epistemology. In L. Alcoff & E. Potter (Eds.), **Feminist Epistemologies** (pp. 49 - 82). New York and London: Routledge.

Hillier, Y., & Jameson, J. (2003). **Empowering researchers in further education**. Stoke on Trent: Trentham Books.

Lather, P. (1986). "Research as Praxis." **Harvard Educational Review,** 56(3), 257-277.

Leonelli, E., Merson, M. W., Schmitt, M. J., & members of the Massachusetts ABE Math Team (Eds.). (1994). **The ABE math standards project. Volume 2: implementing the Massachusetts adult basic education math standards: our research stories**. Holyoke, Massachusetts: Holyoke Community College SABES Regional Center.

Lerman, S. (1998). Research on Socio-Cultural Perspectives of Mathematics Teaching and Learning. In A. Sierpinska & J. Kilpatrick (Eds.), **Mathematics education as a research domain: a search for identity** (pp. 333-350). Dordrecht: Kluwer Academic Publishers.

Lerman, S. (2000). The social turn in mathematics education research. In J. Boaler (Ed.), **Multiple perspectives on mathematics teaching and learning** (pp. 19-44). Westport Connecticut: Ablex Publishing.

Malcolm, J., & Zukas, M. (2000). Becoming an educator: communities of practice in higher education. In I. McNay (Ed.), **Higher Education and its Communities**. Buckingham: SRHE and Open University Press.

Malcolm, J., & Zukas, M. (2001). "Bridging pedagogic gaps: conceptual discontinuities in higher education." **Teaching in Higher Education,** 6(1), 33 - 42.

Moll, L. C. (Ed.). (1992). **Vygotsky and Education: Instructional implications and applications of sociohistorical psychology**. Cambridge: Cambridge University Press.

Moll, L. C., & Greenberg, J. B. (1992). Creating zones of possibilities: Combining social contexts for instruction. In L. C. Moll (Ed.), **Vygotsky and Education: Instructional implications and applications of sociohistorical psychology** (pp. 319 - 348). Cambridge: Cambridge University Press.

Nuñes, T., Light, P., & Mason, J. (1993). "Tools for thought: The measurement of length and area." **Learning and Instruction**, 3, 39-54.

Pheasey, A., Fofonoff, A., Morgan, D., Malicky, G., Keam, L., Norton, M., Park, V., & (Eds.) Mary Norton and Grace Malicky. (2000). **Learning about Participatory Approaches in Adult Literacy Education: Six Research in Practice Studies**. Edmonton, Canada: Learning at the Centre Press.

Somekh, B. (2003). "Theory and Passion in Action Research." **Educational Action Research,** 11(2), 247-264.

Sommerlad, E. (2003). "Theory, research and practice - the problematic appearance of 'pedagogy' in post-compulsory education." **Journal of Adult and Continuing Education,** 8(3), 147-164.

Tomlin, A. (2001a). **Participatory approaches to work with adult basic mathematics students.** Unpublished PHD thesis, King's College London, London.

Tomlin, A. (2001b). 'We become experts': working with basic education students as researchers. In L. Richardson & M. Wolfe (Eds.), **Principles and practice of informal education: Learning through life** (pp. 222-235). London: Routledge.

Tusting, K., & Barton, D. (2003). **Models of adult learning: a literature review** [.pdf file]. National Research and Development Centre for adult literacy and numeracy. Retrieved 17 December, 2003, from the World Wide Web:

Appendix 5

The research team

We chose to advertise for teacher-researchers rather than approach particular sites; we advertised nationally, but received applications only from the London region. We then negotiated with the selected teacher-researchers' employers and were fortunate that all agreed to release their staff for (about) 40 days a year over two years.

The three teacher-researchers initially appointed were Mark Baxter (HMP[2] Brixton), Eamonn Leddy (Westminster Kingsway College) and Liz Richards (Lambeth College). During the first year Mark Baxter moved from the prison to Lambeth College, with released time for a term covering Liz Richards' absence. The teacher-researcher vacancy created by Mark's move was filled by Topo Wresniwiro (HMP Belmarsh). Meanwhile Mark also worked, part-time, in evening courses (South Thames College, with permission but no paid release for the project); and during the second year Eamonn moved to another college (City and Islington College), which agreed to continue his release. So the project had four teacher-researchers (three at any one time), who worked in four Colleges of Further Education (FE) and two prisons, all in Greater London.

The other team members were Alison Tomlin (King's College London), researcher; Diana Coben (Nottingham University/NRDC), principal investigator; and Margaret Brown (King's College London), who co-directed the project.

---

2 HMP: Her Majesty's Prison

List of materials available on the website

Teaching and learning common measures especially at entry level: additional reports and resources

In addition to this report, the project produced materials to support teaching and learning. They are available on the NRDC website: www.nrdc.org.uk/measures

Resources for students and teachers

These are copyright free; readers may adapt them to suit their own contexts.

- Worksheets giving ideas for comparatively open-ended work on measures.
- A scheme of work for an entry level 3 numeracy course, putting measures at the centre, and an example of the use of the measurement of length as a context for work on linear equations.
- Reading materials on the history of measures.
- Examples of entry level examination questions on measures, with a commentary on their ambiguity and complexity.
- Interview transcripts which illustrate the project's data sources and may also be a useful starting point for discussions among students and teachers.
- Notes from a discussion with a group of ESOL students about the words used in questions about measures.
- A collection of problems to do with measures, including closed and more open questions, which may be used as a starting point for discussion with students about which sorts of problems they prefer.
- Links to selected other resources.